D0207064

Library

THE BEDFORD SERIES IN HISTORY AND CULTURE

The Trial of
Mary Queen of Scots

A Brief History with Documents

Related Titles in
THE BEDFORD SERIES IN HISTORY AND CULTURE
Advisory Editors: Lynn Hunt, *University of California, Los Angeles*
David W. Blight, *Yale University*
Bonnie G. Smith, *Rutgers University*
Natalie Zemon Davis, *Princeton University*
Ernest R. May, *Harvard University*

DA
787
.A1
L625
1999

The Trial of Mary Queen of Scots

A Brief History with Documents

Jayne Elizabeth Lewis

University of California, Los Angeles

BEDFORD/ST. MARTIN'S   Boston   New York

acm 40923058
Santiago Canyon College
Library

For Bedford/St. Martin's
History Editor: Katherine Kurzman
Developmental Editor: Louise Townsend
Editorial Assistant: Molly Kalkstein
Production Supervisor: Paula Keller
Marketing Manager: Charles Cavaliere
Project Management: Books By Design, Inc.
Index: Books By Design, Inc.
Text Design: Claire Seng-Niemoeller
Cover Design: Donna Dennison
Cover Photo: Anonymous, *Mary Queen of Scots,* Victoria and Albert Museum, London, Great Britain.
Composition: ComCom, an R. R. Donnelley & Sons Company
Printing and Binding: Haddon Craftsmen, an R. R. Donnelley & Sons Company

President: Charles H. Christensen
Editorial Director: Joan E. Feinberg
Director of Editing, Design, and Production: Marcia Cohen
Editor in Chief: Nancy Perry
Manager, Publishing Services: Emily Berleth

Library of Congress Catalog Card Number: 98-86157

Copyright © 1999 by Bedford/St. Martin's

All rights reserved. No part of this book may be reproduced, stored in a retrieval system, or transmitted in any form or by any means, electronic, mechanical, photocopying, recording, or otherwise, except as may be expressly permitted by the applicable copyright statutes or in writing by the Publisher.

Manufactured in the United States of America.

7 6
f e d c

For information, write: Bedford / St. Martin's, 75 Arlington Street, Boston, MA 02116 (617-399-4000)

ISBN-10: 0-312-15439-9 (paperback)
        0-312-21815-X (hardcover)
ISBN-13: 978-0-312-15439-4

Photo Credits
Page 47, By courtesy of the National Portrait Gallery, London; page 48, By courtesy of the National Portrait Gallery, London; page 50, The Royal Collection © Her Majesty Queen Elizabeth II; page 51, By permission of the British Library; page 52, By permission of the Blairs Museum Trustees, Aberdeen.

Foreword

The Bedford Series in History and Culture is designed so that readers can study the past as historians do.

The historian's first task is finding the evidence. Documents, letters, memoirs, interviews, pictures, movies, novels, or poems can provide facts and clues. Then the historian questions and compares the sources. There is more to do than in a courtroom, for hearsay evidence is welcome, and the historian is usually looking for answers beyond act and motive. Different views of an event may be as important as a single verdict. How a story is told may yield as much information as what it says.

Along the way the historian seeks help from other historians and perhaps from specialists in other disciplines. Finally, it is time to write, to decide on an interpretation and how to arrange the evidence for readers.

Each book in this series contains an important historical document or group of documents, each document a witness from the past and open to interpretation in different ways. The documents are combined with some element of historical narrative—an introduction or a biographical essay, for example—that provides students with an analysis of the primary source material and important background information about the world in which it was produced.

Each book in the series focuses on a specific topic within a specific historical period. Each provides a basis for lively thought and discussion about several aspects of the topic and the historian's role. Each is short enough (and inexpensive enough) to be a reasonable one-week assignment in a college course. Whether as classroom or personal reading, each book in the series provides firsthand experience of the challenge—and fun—of discovering, recreating, and interpreting the past.

Lynn Hunt
David W. Blight
Bonnie G. Smith
Natalie Zemon Davis
Ernest R. May

Preface

Mary Stuart, Queen of Scots, was beheaded in 1587 because she was deemed an intolerable threat to the state and person of her illustrious cousin once-removed, Elizabeth I. The controversial treason trial that preceded and justified her execution not only introduced the final chapter of Mary's eventful life but also stands in its own right as an illuminating record of political, religious, moral, and psychological tension at a formative moment in modern European history. This volume explores that moment, interweaving the voices of Mary, Elizabeth, and their contemporaries to give the modern reader access to a range of controversies and dilemmas whose meaning reverberates to the present day.

Though a claimant to the English throne, Mary was half French and Roman Catholic, a wife three times over, and a mother as well, with strong ties to the European continent; she was deposed from her own Scottish throne in 1567 and spent nineteen years as a captive of the Elizabethan state. The famously virginal Elizabeth was by contrast Protestant and wholly English, the key to political and religious cohesion in her country. The troubled relationship between these two queens, culminating in Mary's trial and execution, both shaped and was shaped by the volatile domestic and European politics of the day; it also became a focal point for religious conflict in the century following the Protestant Reformation. Meanwhile, Mary's one great similarity to Elizabeth—her sex—made her the center of contemporary dispute over the legitimacy and desirability of female rule. Anyone interested in the cultural and political formation of modern England, or in the religious controversies, European relations, and sexual politics of the Elizabethan period, will be drawn to an extraordinary episode in the life of sixteenth-century Europe.

Elizabeth herself dubbed Mary "the daughter of debate," and this documentary history incorporates texts involved in several contemporary debates—between Protestants and Catholics, between supporters and critics of female rule, between Elizabeth and Mary, between Mary and her English tribunal, between Elizabeth and her own Parliament, and even between different sides of Elizabeth herself. By bringing all of these texts into dialogue with one another, *The Trial of Mary Queen of Scots* spotlights several of the "debate[s]" regarding whose "daughter" Mary was, and even allows the modern reader to participate in them. The world of Mary Stuart and Elizabeth Tudor was a complex and difficult one, at last lacking in both villains and heroines. This volume is meant to foster both critical and sympathetic appreciation of that fact.

Following an introduction that explores and illuminates several of these debates, this volume reprints excerpts from two sixteenth-century treatises on the legitimacy of female rule, John Knox's *The First Blast of the Trumpet against the Monstrous Regiment of Women* (1558) and John Leslie's *A Defence of the Honour of . . . Marie* (1569), along with part of George Buchanan's scathing ad-feminem attack against Mary Stuart, *Ane Detection of the Doings of Mary Queen of Scots* (1571). The record of Mary's trial is flanked on one side by some of her letters to and from Elizabeth and by the Bond of Association, the legal document that paved the way to it; and on the other by Elizabeth's riddling speeches to Parliament following Mary's conviction of treason against the English crown. Finally, two competing versions of Mary's execution — Robert Wyngfield's eyewitness account and an excerpt from Adam Blackwood's *History of Mary Queen of Scots* (1587) — show how Mary Stuart continued to create conflicts of interpretation and belief even after her death.

ACKNOWLEDGMENTS

Many people have kept the editing of this volume from being, itself, a trial. Foremost among them is Brook Thomas, who not only sparked the thought of such a project but stoked its fires through many months of research and writing. I am also especially grateful to my research assistant, Johanna Schwartz, and to Andy Kelly for his unflagging interest in the sorrows of Mary Queen of Scots. I owe much to the rigorous readings of Constance Jordan, Carole Levin, Catherine Patterson, Benjamin Schmidt, Malcolm Smuts, and Johann P. Sommerville. Two of my colleagues at UCLA, Lowell Gallagher and Claire McEachern, have always enriched and encouraged my engagement with the Elizabethans, while Maryclaire Moroney has been a loyal and stimulating partner in arms from Edinburgh to the Isle of Skye.

In many ways, my greatest debt is to my development editor at Bedford, Louise Townsend, who has shared her gifts of tact, exactitude, and sheer intelligence so generously throughout. Thanks as well to Katherine Kurzman, Chuck Christensen, and Joan Feinberg, to Molly Kalkstein for superb editorial assistance, and to my production editor, Emily Berleth. A grant from the National Endowment for the Humanities gave me the time and space to complete this project, and, as ever, my parents, Eldon and Stella Lewis, remain my first resource and final refuge.

Jayne Elizabeth Lewis

Contents

THE BEDFORD SERIES IN HISTORY AND CULTURE

The Trial of Mary Queen of Scots

A Brief History with Documents

PART ONE

Introduction:
Two Queens and a Crown

On a February morning in 1587, a most extraordinary event took place at the isolated English castle of Fotheringay: Mary Stuart, anointed queen of neighboring Scotland and dowager queen of France, crossed a crowded room to kneel at a scaffold that had been hammered together the night before. Sumptuously dressed and radiantly calm, the Roman Catholic Queen of Scots murmured a psalm in Latin; as she fell silent, an ax descended to separate her carefully dressed head from her graceful neck. After two more blows had completed the task, a cloth was ripped from a nearby billiard table, and in that shroud the queen's body was stored away, to be buried only six months later at the local cathedral of Peterborough. Meanwhile, all bloody traces of the execution were consigned to the flames. Church bells pealed to proclaim the demise of the woman who had been a thorn in England's side for most of her forty-four years.

In London, one-hundred miles to the south, another queen greeted news of the thorn's extraction with mixed emotions. Elizabeth Tudor, England's ruler for the last twenty-nine years, had reluctantly signed the warrant for Mary's death a few months before, just after a short but dramatic state trial had found the Queen of Scots guilty of conspiring to kill

1

Elizabeth and usurp her throne. For one monarch to order the execution of another was unprecedented,[1] but Elizabeth's action had at least lowered the curtain on a decades-long tragedy that in its time involved not only the two queens but also their bordering countries and even their churches, Roman Catholic and Protestant. Yet although Mary had long stood as her most formidable rival, Elizabeth, now the lone female ruler in all of Europe, could not feel simple relief at her bloody end. The two queens had also been cousins (once-removed) and, although they had never met, their lives had run parallel courses. The death of the woman she had sometimes even called sister was the death of part of Elizabeth as well.

The four-month period that began with Mary's treason trial and ended with her beheading comprises a pivotal episode in English history. In turn, the numerous and rich records that this episode generated give us an extraordinary glimpse into sixteenth-century England's turbulent political, religious, and even psychological life. On the surface, that life looks singularly sunny. Elizabeth Tudor, whose rule lasted until 1603, was dearly beloved and by almost any standard the most successful monarch that England had ever known. During the golden reign of "Gloriana," her country attained an impressive level of political and religious stability, cultural brilliance, and international prestige.[2] Aided by an expanding trade network and a literary tradition that projected a glowing and confident national image, a backward island under Elizabeth shrugged off its medieval chrysalis to emerge as a modern state of the first magnitude. In less than two centuries' time, its empire would span the globe.

Contemporary portraits of Queen Elizabeth (Figure 1) show England's splendor embodied in her. But such proud preeminence was far from secure or inevitable, and the path to it was never easy or straight, especially in the first decades of Elizabeth's reign. On the contrary, just under an ever-more-resplendent veneer seethed a viper's nest of crises and conflicts — over the nature of monarchy, over the specific desirability of female rule, over England's religious identity, and even over its status and survival among the other kingdoms of Western Europe. In part because Mary Queen of Scots came to stand for everything that Elizabeth

---

[1] It is true that the executions of two kings had been ordered in England's past: Henry IV had called for the death of Richard II in 1400, and Edward IV for that of Henry VI in 1483. But Henry IV and Edward IV were crowned only after the demises of their predecessors; Elizabeth remained the first sitting monarch to sign a warrant for the death of another sovereign.

[2] "Gloriana" is the adulatory name the poet Edmund Spenser gave Elizabeth in his long allegory dedicated to her, *The Faerie Queene* (1590–96).

Queen of England was not, the relationship between the two women was molded by these conflicts. When Mary came to trial for treason on October 15, 1586, many matters of dispute seemed close to resolution, and when she knelt at the scaffold on February 8, 1587 they even appeared to have been resolved. But a close look at the documents of the trial in their context yields a different view of England's history, suggesting less a nation's steady and inexorable progress to glory than a series of interminable struggles waged in an atmosphere of passion, fear, and mystery.

THE ROAD TO FOTHERINGAY

Tudor Quandaries

Elizabeth Tudor came to the English throne in 1558, very much against the odds. Although her father had been King Henry VIII, one of England's most forceful and dynamic rulers ever, her mother had been his scandal-ridden second wife, Anne Boleyn. After fathering a daughter with his first, devoutly Catholic, wife, Catherine of Aragon, Henry—desperate for a male heir—had divorced her for Anne. To do so, he had had to repudiate England's official Roman Catholic faith, establishing the Church of England as the state religion in its stead.[3]

Though he had seemingly moved heaven and earth to marry her, Henry soon tired of Anne Boleyn, and not long after the birth of yet another daughter, Elizabeth, he found several pretexts—treason and adultery chief among them—to have his second wife beheaded. Henry declared their baby a bastard, and in this, at least, the Roman Catholic Church concurred, since Catherine of Aragon had still been alive at the child's conception. Elizabeth was thus bound to grow up under the shadow of her mother's sullied name, barely acknowledged by a father whose attentions soon centered on the one son he managed to produce, with his third wife, Jane Seymour.

After Henry's death in 1547, the crown passed to this son, the sickly Edward VI, and upon Edward's early death in 1553 to Mary Tudor, Henry's daughter by Catherine of Aragon. An even more fervent Catholic than her mother had been, Mary was also the wife of Philip, prince of Catholic Spain. And in her zeal to bring England back into the fold of the

---

[3]The state church that Henry established remained in many ways Catholic in its traditions and doctrines; indeed, it did not discard the Catholic Mass until 1549. At that time, under Henry's son Edward VI, the Church of England became Protestant, but even today it is more hierarchical—and closer in spirit to the Catholic Church—than any other Protestant denomination.

true church, she persecuted her own Protestant subjects so vigorously that she has gone down in history under the unflattering epithet of "Bloody Mary." Predictably, Mary Tudor's short but gory reign fostered suspicion and enmity between English Protestants and their Catholic counterparts. The latter often viewed Protestants as upstarts and heretics, while many Protestants associated the Roman Catholic Church with bitter tyranny, at the same time fearing any tie to the Catholic powers of continental Europe that might jeopardize the integrity and independence of their own small country.

Nor was their fear unfounded. While the Protestant Reformation earlier in the sixteenth century had already challenged the Roman Catholic hegemony of medieval times, Western Europe remained divided between two formidable Catholic dynasties—the Hapsburgs, who ruled Spain, and the Valois kings of France. Though challenged by Protestant movements at home, both of these power blocks were already busy extending their conquests in the New World across the Atlantic, and alongside them England looked like a feeble scrap of soil, one almost as ripe for the taking as the lands of North and South America. Despite England's sizable Protestant population, its queen's marriage to Philip of Spain thus yoked it to Hapsburg Europe with a violence that often seemed to guarantee both Catholic and Spanish domination in the future.

Mary Tudor's bloody stint on England's throne fueled other anxieties as well. Apart from those revolving around questions of religious and political identity, one of the deepest concerned the scope and nature of sovereign power. At the time of Mary's accession, her subjects imagined that power in forms inherited from the medieval past and considered it to be enormous. By and large, the prevailing notion of royal prerogative stemmed from the doctrine of the king's two bodies. In place for centuries, this doctrine held that monarchs in effect possessed two bodies, one natural and one political. The king's body natural was his physical body, subject to decay and mortality, but accorded certain powers that were absolute in the sense that they need not conform to law or custom. His body "politic" was a more mystical entity; it was attached to the body natural, but unlike that body did not die. Instead, it passed from individual king to individual king, all the while enjoying numerous temporal privileges in conjunction with Parliament.[4]

At least as important as the empowering concept of the king's two bod-

[4]Ernst Kantorowicz's *The King's Two Bodies* (Princeton: Princeton University Press, 1957) is the classic work on this subject. In *The Queen's Two Bodies: Drama and the Elizabethan Succession* (London: Royal Historical Society, 1977), Marie Axton applies some of Kantorowicz's model to the special case of Elizabeth Tudor.

ico was that of his divine appointment. A monarch's very touch was believed to possess the power of sacred healing, and his will was presumably aligned with God's.[5] But by Mary Tudor's time, belief in that alignment had come under attack from several quarters. There was, for example, the troublesome precedent of Henry VIII himself, who despite his marital escapades and cavalier manipulations of power—especially in the repudiation of papal authority—had grown more and more dependent on his Parliament. Henry had given members of that body's upper House (of Lords) and its lower one (of Commons) an important role in the question of succession outside the Tudor family; he depended on their support in the creation and maintenance of the Church of England; and above all he needed Parliament in the delicate matter of taxation. The royal coffers were never very full, and, in a tradition that would outlive him, Henry relied on the revenues brought in by the constituencies of individual members of Parliament.

What's more, while still largely concentrated in the hands of the landed peerage and gentry, English wealth had by the 1550s begun to migrate to the urban merchant and entrepreneurial classes. Some of the members of these classes happened also to belong to the lower houses of Parliament and thus wielded considerable political power. Many of them were of the new Protestant faith, whose emphasis on the endeavors and entitlements of the individual supported capitalist enterprise. Although Catholics too were involved in entrepreneurial activity, it remained that the more communally oriented church of Rome had grown up entwined with feudal society. A new distribution of wealth and influence, sometimes reinforced by religious ideology, was bound to challenge the hierarchical, semimystical assumptions of England's Catholic past . . . and, in time, the authority of the Catholic queen, Mary Tudor.

But Mary's royal prerogative was perhaps most gravely undermined by the simple fact that she was a woman. In English society women possessed no political authority of any description. Just as the Book of Genesis depicted Eve as Adam's subordinate, so was woman construed as man's inferior. Women's lower status was difficult to reconcile with the obvious supremacy of the monarchy, especially since as queen of England Mary Tudor also headed its church, and the influential Christian apostle St. Paul had explicitly prohibited women from priesthood. Then, too, women's uniquely inescapable reproductive lives seemed to root

[5]Mary Tudor actually revived several old rituals meant to assert a king's divinity—a strategy that, according to Carole Levin, betrays the vulnerability of her own position. See Levin "'Would I Could Give You Help and Succour': Elizabeth I and the Politics of Touch," *Albion* 21 (1989): 91–205.

them permanently in the physical world. Contaminated by that world's mutability, frail and unpredictable, they seemed to many incapable of the clean separation of being that made the doctrine of the king's two bodies possible. Though it certainly included examples of patriotic and godly heroines like Esther and Deborah, the Old Testament itself offered the powerful cautionary figure of the sensual and bloodthirsty harlot queen Jezebel. But even without Jezebel's precedent, common contempt for the female body would have conspired with the popular assumption that, because she was naturally disorderly and in need of constraint by man, woman should never reign over man. That conspiracy could prevent even a princess of the blood from inheriting indisputable authority with her crown.[6]

When Mary Tudor died, childless, in 1558, she thus left a country torn by religious fear and animosity, one at best unpersuaded by female rule and increasingly skeptical about the sovereign-worshipping social hierarchies of the past.[7] She also left an England embroiled in conflict with the neighbor to its immediate north, Scotland. Today Scotland and England, along with Wales and Northern Ireland, are part of the United Kingdom. But in the sixteenth century the two countries clung to very separate identities and were ruled by different monarchs. England had long sought to dominate a smaller and less populous kingdom, one that defiantly preserved its own "auld Alliance" with the Valois power block of Catholic Europe. The Scottish king, Henry's contemporary James V, had even married a French woman, Marie de Guise, and the French often supported Scotland against the English.[8] In part because the "auld Alliance" threatened to open the door to a French invasion of England, Henry VIII

---

[6]Belief in women's permanent internal confusion stemmed from uncontrollable bodily processes such as menstruation and pregnancy, but was often countered by the conviction of female modesty and inherent delicacy. Natalie Davis presents both sides in "Woman on Top," in Davis, *Society and Culture in Early Modern France* (Stanford: Stanford University Press, 1975), 124–51. Constance Jordan relates such notions of feminine subjugation directly to arguments against women's rule in "Women's Rule in Sixteenth-Century British Thought," *Renaissance Quarterly* 40 (1991): 421–52.

[7]Historians disagree about the extent of antimonarchical feeling in the late Tudor period. J. E. Neale tried to establish its ascendancy in his classic *Elizabeth and Her Parliaments* (London: Jonathan Cape, 1957), but his argument has been tempered by scholars like Geoffrey Elton. See Elton's essay, "Parliament," in Christopher Haigh, ed., *The Reign of Elizabeth I* (London: Macmillan, 1984), 79–100. It is generally conceded, however, that by the second half of the sixteenth century, Parliament had become more powerful than it had been in the past.

[8]Within France, the family of Marie de Guise (who is sometimes called Marie de Lorraine) was actually a threat to the Valois dynasty, but this complication did not make Scotland's ties to Catholic France seem any less a menace to the Protestant English and their Scottish sympathizers and co-religionists.

had tried to arrange a marriage between his son, Edward VI, and James's infant daughter, Mary Stuart. When that plan failed, he aimed to beat Scotland into submission by raiding and burning its ports and cities.

This "rough wooing" (as the novelist Sir Walter Scott was to call it) finally drove the Scottish royal family full into the arms of the French. Mary Stuart was betrothed to the French dauphin, and her country remained a battleground between English and French interests. Scots themselves were divided: Though many approved of the "auld Alliance," a powerful subgroup loyal to England emerged in the 1540s and 1550s, in tandem with a growing Protestant movement whose adherents were often more strictly Calvinist than were members of the Church of England.

Though each one is distinct, the tensions we have just considered often collided. For example, one of the sixteenth century's most outspoken enemies of female rule, John Knox, was a Scottish Presbyterian, a bearded demagogue who preached the monstrosity of the "regiment of women" with the same bitter and impassioned eloquence he used to denounce the Catholic Church. An excerpt from Knox's most fulsome tirade on the subject, *The First Blast of the Trumpet against the Monstrous Regiment of Women* (1558), appears in Document 1. Knox anchored his twofold argument against female sovereignty, or gynecocracy, both in "Nature" and in holy scripture. *The First Blast* thus cites numerous passages from the Old and New Testaments that place woman below man, while also claiming that "Nature hath in all beasts printed a certain mark of dominion in the male, and a certain subjection in the female." Once he had established the "fact" that the complementary laws of nature and holy writ made female rule a "monstrous" deviation from the right hierarchy of things, Knox could declare gynecocracy a species of treason: "For that woman reigneth above man, she hath obtained it by treason and conspiracy committed against God" (Document 1).

In the end, Mary Tudor's death might have rendered Knox's point moot (at least in England) had not her heir apparent turned out to be yet another woman. At twenty-five, Mary's half sister, Elizabeth, was Protestant in her religious convictions, toughened by years of adversity that had even included a short captivity, and far more shrewd than either of her siblings had been. To survive, Elizabeth had already perfected the art of playing her supporters against one another, simultaneously agreeing with all and none while carefully veiling her own motives and intentions. She was to hone these skills over the course of her reign; indeed, they became the key to her political survival.

For example, at the time of her accession, Elizabeth's subjects fully expected her to marry. Early portraits of her as queen (Figure 2) depicted her with her hair down, suggesting a virgin on the brink of marriage.[9] But while her people earnestly wished for her to produce an heir, Elizabeth nimbly sidestepped any number of prospective husbands, even those who had the backing of many of her most powerful subjects. Over time, it became apparent that the queen had little intention of taking a husband. Indeed, after an apparent fling with one of her favorites threatened to compromise her reputation, she was happy to let the image of virginal purity crystallize around her. In the long run, that image became one of Elizabeth's most potent weapons, for it allowed her to present herself as espoused to her people, even as she remained independent of individual men in a way that a married woman of her time could not hope to be. Then, too, Elizabeth's avoidance of marriage kept England out from under the thumb of other European countries, and it countered popular mistrust of the dangerously mixed nature of the sexualized woman. Although Elizabeth never entirely escaped rumor and innuendo, the myth of chaste maidenhood held fast and on the whole served her remarkably well. At the very least, that myth helped the queen to steer clear of the imputations that had shadowed her mother, Anne Boleyn, who had after all been branded a whore and beheaded accordingly.

The Mary Stuart Menace

But Elizabeth had to contend with a shadow even more menacing than that of Anne Boleyn. Her subjects turned out to be far from unanimous in their support. To some—and especially to those of the Roman Catholic persuasion—the fact that both her own father and the pope had declared her a bastard canceled her title to the throne. Next in *legitimate* line, they held, was another Mary—Mary Stuart, fifteen-year-old queen of Scotland at the time of Elizabeth's accession and, as it happened, just married to the crown prince of France as well.

Mary Stuart's grandmother had been Margaret Tudor, sister of Henry VIII, who had married Scotland's king, James IV, and given birth to Mary's father, James V. Her mother was Marie de Guise, daughter of one of the most powerful families in Catholic France. (See family tree, Fig-

[9]Readers curious about the ways Elizabeth manipulated her own virginity—and the ways in which that image could on occasion backfire—should consult Helen Hackett, *Virgin Mother, Maiden Queen* (London: Macmillan, 1995). Hackett is especially concerned to show the complications of Elizabeth's legendary virginity, as is Philippa Berry in *Of Chastity and Power* (Oxford: Oxford University Press, 1993). For a more straightforward assessment of Elizabeth as virgin queen, see Frances Yates, *Astraea: The Imperial Theme in the Sixteenth Century* (London: Routledge, 1975), and Roy Strong, *The Cult of Elizabeth: Elizabethan Portraiture and Pageantry* (London: Thames and Hudson, 1977).

ure 3.) Sterling at least in point of legitimacy, this pedigree, to many minds, placed Mary before Elizabeth in line to the throne. Yet, Henry VIII had left a will excluding the Stuart line from the English succession, and Elizabeth's supporters brandished it at every opportunity. Recalling common law strictures barring those of foreign birth from positions of power in England, they also pointed to Mary's French blood, as well as to the fact that she had been born on Scottish rather than on English soil. And it is they who carried the day, especially since Mary Stuart was a Catholic, just like the recently departed Mary Tudor, once hated and feared by so many.[10]

Relieved to have escaped Mary Tudor's oppressive yoke and determined never again to suffer under Catholic rule, most Protestant Englishmen supported Elizabeth's ascent to the throne. Others came out on her side after they weighed their distaste for female rule against a general belief in hereditary right and the relatively clear lack of appropriate male claimants. In the end, Elizabeth was crowned with exceptional, if not unanimous, support from her weary subjects and at her coronation she kissed a copy of the Great Bible—an English-language version of the Old and New Testaments that had become a potent symbol of a Protestant England.[11]

Nonetheless, Mary Stuart still posed a serious threat both to England's makeshift unity of political affection and to Elizabeth's personal authority. First, there was the question that Mary's very existence raised: Was she or was she not foreign? If she was in fact an alien, could she then inherit the crown?[12] What, in other words, was Scotland's relationship to England? As an ostensibly rougher and politically weaker country, was

---

[10]These matters, including the controversy over Henry VIII's codicil, are taken up by Mortimer Levine in both *The Early Elizabethan Succession Question* (Stanford: Stanford University Press, 1966) and *Tudor Dynastic Problems, 1460–1571* (London: Allen and Unwin, 1973), 74–75, 99. Elizabeth did have other rivals besides Mary, including Lady Margaret Lennox and her son Henry Lennox, Lord Darnley, and Lady Katherine Grey, but their claims paled beside those of Mary, whose Continental ties also made her far more significant than other competitors for the throne.

[11]In general, the Protestants placed the authority of scripture over the ritual and visual symbolism of the Roman Catholic Church. The Great Bible was first published in 1539, with Henry VIII on the title page; after Elizabeth came to the throne, she replaced her father there, and the Great Bible's successor, the Bishops' Bible of 1569, features her as the defender of the Protestant faith. See John King, *Tudor Royal Iconography* (Princeton: Princeton University Press, 1989), 16–17.

[12]This question was floated most widely in John Hales's influential 1563 *Treatise*, in *Treatises in the Hereditary Right of the Crowne of England*, ed. G. Harbin (London, 1713). The matter of Henry's will was pursued by Edmund Plowden in 1566. For detailed discussion of these texts and their arguments, see Marie Axton, "The Influence of Edmund Plowden's Succession Treatise," *Huntington Library Quarterly* 37 (1974): 209–26.

it England's subordinate and therefore part of it? Certainly, many contended that it was, holding that the kings of Scotland had long acknowledged "the king of England to be the superior lord over the realm of Scotland."[13] On the other hand, wouldn't anointing a Scottish-born queen in effect subject England to its supposed inferior? There was also the troubling fact of Scotland's "auld Alliance" with a strong and Catholic France. The question that Mary Stuart raised, of whether England's own boundaries properly encompassed those of Scotland (or, for that matter, France's those of England), opened the way to deeper philosophical quandaries about what was foreign to England and what was not.

In any event, Mary's Frenchness posed a problem unto itself. Although virtually all English historiography refers to her as Mary Stuart, the queen's given name was in fact Marie, and she spoke of herself as such throughout her life. Her native tongue was French, and she had been sent to France at the age of five to be bred in the court of the Valois king, Henri II. Mary almost always wrote and preferred to speak in French. At fifteen she married François II, the French dauphin, later joining him on the French throne until his premature death in 1560.

Mary's Frenchness in turn intersected with two other, equally disconcerting qualities: her Roman Catholic religion and her coquettish personality. The official church of France was Roman Catholic, and the Queen of Scots was devoted to it from earliest childhood. Besides, the French court was notoriously the most sophisticated, if also probably the most decadent, in Europe. There Mary acquired an array of charms and cultivations that, combined with her regal height (of 5'10") and lovely face, made her the darling of the Valois court poets and an extraordinarily seductive presence wherever she went. Throughout her life, Mary managed to beguile even skeptical Englishmen into the admission that she was "the finest she that ever was."[14]

But what made Mary Stuart most alarming to Elizabeth, and in turn to many of that queen's subjects, was that while she was barely in her teens her mother's ambitious brothers had joined with the king of France himself in urging her to claim the arms of England as her own. The Guises were merely eager for a political toehold in England, but their impressionable niece absorbed their belief in her own entitlement. In short, Mary promised an England quite unlike the one that came into being under her cousin once-removed. To imagine Mary was to imagine

[13]John Leslie, *A Defence of the Honour of . . . Marie* (London, 1569), 66.
[14]Thomas Randolph to William Cecil, Lord Burghley, *Calendar of State Papers Relating to Scotland and Mary Queen of Scots (CSP, Scot.)* (Edinburgh, 1880–1969), II:229.

England's shadow self—Catholic rather than Protestant in its dominant religious inclinations, and intimately bound to the powerful Valois sector of continental Europe instead of proudly independent of it.

Nor did Mary's differences from Elizabeth end with her religion and cultural affiliation. Whereas the Tudor queen, as we have seen, was increasingly concerned to preserve a protective image of virginal purity, Mary was married before she was halfway through her teens. Upon her first husband's death, she returned to her own country to resume her throne, clad in the white veil of mourning, traditional in France, that was to become her signature (Figure 4). In time she made a second marriage, this time to a "handsome, bearded and lady-faced" English Catholic, Henry, Lord Darnley.[15] Since wives were deemed subordinate to their husbands, Mary's marriage alone complicated any attempt to grant her the unrivalled status of a queen. To make matters worse, she was rumored to have wed Darnley out of sexual lust. At the very least, Mary's eventful sexual history meant that whereas the unmarried Elizabeth was usually able to hold herself apart from dangerous stereotypes about female emotionality, sexuality, and vulnerability, the Queen of Scots was doomed to play into them.

Perhaps most notably, however, Elizabeth was an adroit manipulator of her own ministers, and her willingness to involve herself in politics actually reinforced the sovereign authority in which she so deeply believed. By contrast, although Mary had been Scotland's queen virtually all her life (her father, James V, having died when she was six days old), she lacked real, hard political experience, and indeed displayed a singular lack of interest in acquiring it. While Mary was still living a sheltered life in France, her mother was adroitly managing Scotland on her behalf. And upon Marie de Guise's death in 1560, the reins of government fell into the hands of Mary's half brother—her father's illegitimate son, James, Earl of Moray.

The clever and ambitious Moray befriended a growing coalition of Protestant lords, many of whom subscribed to John Knox's vituperative views on both female rule and the Catholic faith. Suspicious of Continental ways, contemptuous of her ability to govern, and fearful that Mary would persecute Scottish Protestants as Mary Tudor had persecuted English ones, many of Mary's Protestant lords, led by Moray, made her life impossibly difficult from the moment she came back from France. And Mary,

---

[15]James Melville, *Memoirs of Sir James Melville,* ed. A. Francis Steuart (New York: Dutton, 1930), 92.

while believing as devoutly as Elizabeth in her own royal privilege, fatally avoided involving herself deeply in affairs of state.[16]

Despite their differences, Mary Stuart and Elizabeth Tudor nonetheless shared one overwhelming, if obvious, similarity: Both were women. And thanks to the Salic law that kept women from the French throne, as well as to similar rules of exclusion in many other European countries, they were the only two who ruled in Europe.[17] But while it ought to have brought them together, the fact that both rulers were female actually compounded the stress of their relationship. On the surface that relationship was normally civil and often even affectionate; underneath lurked Elizabeth's fear that Mary would challenge her throne, and Mary's resentment of Elizabeth's habit of interfering with her own authority. "You be tender cousins, both Queens in the flower of your ages, much resembling other in most excellent and goodly qualities," Moray wrote to Elizabeth. "But your sex will not permit you to advance your glory."[18]

Elizabeth's enormously influential Secretary of State, William Cecil, was especially astute about the real problems that stemmed from the fact that Mary and Elizabeth were "two queens in one isle," neither able to trust the other fully, yet each dependent on the other, and both bearing the burden of power in an age reluctant to grant it to women. "God could not have blessed these two kingdoms with greater felicity, than if one of the two queens had been a king," he wrote.[19] Another of Elizabeth's ministers, Nicholas Throckmorton, echoed Cecil when he wished "that one of these two Queens of the isle of Britain were transformed into the shape of a man, to make so happy a marriage, as thereby there might be an unity of the whole isle." Both Cecil and Throckmorton implied that if one of the two queens had been a king, she might have married the other, and Scotland and England would then have been peaceably united. Ideally, Elizabeth would have been the husband king, for then Scotland's subjection to England would have found a perfect mirror in the gendered

---

[16]Jenny Wormald pursues this tendency as the foundation of Mary's political failure throughout *Mary Queen of Scots: A Study in Failure* (London: George Philip, 1988).

[17]At least officially. Catherine de Medici, wife of the French king Henri II, wielded considerable power, even after his death. "Salic law," derived from the code law of the Salian Franks which prohibited female inheritance and barred women from the thrones of France and Spain.

[18]Moray to Elizabeth, August 6, 1561. *CSP, Scot.,* I:540–41. Moray specifies that the queens could only hope to "advance [their] glory" in "a peaceable reign," knowing full well that true peace was unlikely.

[19]William Cecil to Elizabeth. *CSP, Scot.* II:80. The phrase "two queens in one isle" was coined by Mary's uncle Francois, Duc de Guise. For a full commentary on its significance, see Alison Plowden, *Two Queens in One Isle: The Deadly Relationship of Elizabeth I and Mary Queen of Scots* (Sussex: Harvester Press, 1984).

relationship between the two rulers. But since Mary and Elizabeth obviously could not marry, they were forced into incessant competition. For Elizabeth, in particular, this competition was as personal as it was political, and Mary's emissary James Melville took notice. A typical visit to the English queen ended with her asking Melville whether Mary's hair or hers was the lovelier, and "which of them two was fairest," then "which of them was of highest stature." Upon being informed that Mary was, Elizabeth declared that the Queen of Scots was "too high and that herself was neither too high nor too low." She even arranged for Melville to overhear her at the virginals, upon which "she asked whether my queen or she played best." Later, the queen demanded to know "whether she or my queen danced best."[20]

Elizabeth's anxious queries about her cousin once-removed almost comically exaggerate the differences between the two queens—differences that only widened as Mary's second marriage turned out to be a profoundly miserable one. Darnley soon cast his lot with Mary's truculent lords rather than with the queen herself, even plotting with them to stab his wife's beloved Italian secretary, David Rizzio, to death in her presence. Mary was pregnant at the time, and soon she bore a son, the future James VI of Scotland. But her marriage, for obvious reasons, never recovered from the Rizzio incident. Before long, Darnley himself had been murdered, and Mary was suspected of having had a hand in his demise.[21] When shortly after Darnley's death she eloped with the man believed to have done the actual killing—James Hepburn, Earl of Bothwell—she effectively signed her monarchy's death warrant. Led by her half brother Moray, Mary's subjects mounted a rebellion against her. They imprisoned their queen in a castle in the middle of Scotland's desolate Loch Leven and there, in 1567, forced her to resign her crown to her year-old son, James VI. Though Mary later escaped her island prison, and even mounted a briefly successful rally against her own rebellious subjects, she was eventually defeated. She fled to England, hoping for safe harbor and the redress of grievances from her cousin Elizabeth.

The dramatic events that brought an end to Mary's personal rule in Scotland are crucial to an understanding not just of what became of her in England, but also of two issues that were to come to a head in the final months of her life, almost twenty years later. First, there is the matter of female rule: Many of Mary's troubles in Scotland were rooted in the fact that she was a woman. Once she had fallen, the stereotypical brands of

---

[20]Melville, *Memoirs*, 94.

[21]The circumstances of Darnley's death were highly suspicious: While he was recovering from a probable venereal illness in Edinburgh's Kirk o'Field, the building was blown to bits. Darnley's body turned up, strangled but otherwise unscorched, in the garden.

adulteress and whore were liberally applied to her. For example, after Darnley's murder, Mary's enemies circulated a crude caricature featuring the Queen of Scots as a mermaid—a contemporary icon of feminine lasciviousness (Figure 5). And after Mary's flight to England, much was made of an apocryphal cache of love letters and sonnets that she had presumably written to Bothwell during her marriage to Darnley.[22] The better to shred what remained of Mary's reputation, the Scottish scholar George Buchanan wrote the most corrosive diatribe against her to be published in her day. Throughout, Buchanan belabored qualities he believed only a woman would possess: "Such are the natures of some women, especially such as cannot brook the greatness of their own good fortune; they have vehement affections both ways; they love with excess, and hate without measure; and to what side soever they bend, they are not govern'd by advis'd reason, but carried by violent motion."[23]

As we find in the excerpt from Buchanan's *Ane Detection of the Doings of Mary Queen of Scots* that appears as Document 2, Mary's alleged crimes, although never absolutely proven, became an occasion for argument against female sovereignty. Mary herself became living confirmation of all the popular reasons why a woman should not be trusted with the crown. The scandal that surrounded her naturally magnified her danger to Elizabeth, who was after all a woman as well, daughter of a queen beheaded for sexual and political misconduct, and separated by a fine line from the very assumptions and allegations that bedevilled her Stuart cousin. Though infinitely more adept at managing her own image—and ministers—Elizabeth was ultimately as vulnerable as Mary to the imputations and representations of her subjects.

At the same time, however, Mary also prompted passionate defenses of female rule. In 1569, the year after her ignominious defeat at the hands of her own subjects, one of her most loyal supporters, the Catholic priest John Leslie, Bishop of Ross, completed his *Defence of the Honour of . . . Marie.* Though also a personal tribute to Mary, Leslie's *Defence* con-

---

[22]The genuineness of the "casket letters," as they came to be known, is highly debatable. They vanished after an English commission tried Mary for adultery and conspiracy in 1568, and generations of historians have exhausted themselves in controversy about the sonnets and letters, which Mary claimed not to have written but which, if authentic, prove her complicity with Bothwell in Darnley's death. Gordon Donaldson's *The First Trial of Mary Queen of Scots* (London: Batsford, 1969) delves deep into the casket letters controversy, while in *Images of a Queen* (Berkeley: University of California Press, 1964), James E. Phillips explores the propaganda for and against Mary that grew out of that controversy. After centuries of debate, the question of whether the letters were forged—and Mary guilty of adultery and conspiracy to murder—remains open.

[23]George Buchanan, *Ane Detection of the Doings of Mary Queen of Scots* ([1571]; London, 1721), 40.

demned theoretical works like Knox's *First Blast* as a "poisoned pestiferous pamphlet" and registered a claim for the legitimacy of female sovereignty.

Leslie's *Defence* (Document 3) links public animus against the Queen of Scots to hostility to female sovereignty itself. In defending the virtue of the queen, Leslie thus also defends the virtues and rectitude of queenly rule itself. Leslie holds that those who opposed Mary's personal right to any throne "expressly denied and refused *all* womanly government" (emphasis added). Similarly, as he refutes the dictum, derived from Knox, that "the civil regiment of women is repugnant both to the law of nature and to the blood," Leslie shows how slanders against Mary— "feigned and forged reports" against her "virtuous good innocence" and reputation—are symbolic assaults on "God's holy word," launched by those who have "licentiously wreathed and wrested" scripture to make female rule look like a crime against divine law (Document 3).

Leslie's rejoinders to Knox range from the scriptural point that woman "was created to the image of God as well as man," and thus has equal right to political authority, to a head-on collision with Knox's argument that the law of nature prohibits female rule. For Leslie, Knox's interpretation of the law of nature is "counterfeit," a manipulative, manmade fiction that has no relationship whatever to the nonhuman, or prehuman, world of nature.[24] In any case, the fact that Mary Stuart could be used by both sides in the debate about the legitimacy of "womanly government" shows how obsessively contemporary thinking (and feeling) about the nature of monarchy centered on her. It also helps to explain some of Elizabeth's ambivalence toward her controversial cousin—an ambivalence that stemmed from more than Mary's demand to be considered, at the very least, next in line to the English throne. Such practical threats were significant, but the symbolic ones were no less real. Her political weakness made Mary Queen of Scots a testing ground for the legitimacy of female rule; after all, questions about that legitimacy could not comfortably be probed with direct reference to the far more formidable Elizabeth Tudor. In turn, Scottish hostility to Mary shadowed the possibility of similar attacks on Elizabeth.

At the same time, the backlash against Mary only thinly disguised a very different kind of rebellion, this one against monarchical authority itself. George Buchanan had claimed that some women's "vehement affections" made them intuitively despotic rulers. But when Mary's subjects forced her to give up her throne, they directly attacked the power

[24]Jordan explores Leslie's interesting perception that the law of nature is merely a political fiction in "Women's Rule," 444.

of any sovereign, female or male. Indeed, by putting a baby in her place, they were retaining only the faintest illusion of monarchical authority, since for years and years to come Scotland would in effect be ruled by a cadre of its subjects, and not by a sovereign at all.

When Mary fled to England, then, she brought more than one kind of trouble with her. In the first place, she was seen as Elizabeth's rival, one whose Roman Catholic faith and ties to France threatened England's autonomy and its provisional religious identity. Equally important, Mary was a reminder of how precarious Elizabeth's own position was, not just as queen at a time when female sovereignty could be seen as itself an act of treason against God, but as a monarch in an age and culture that found more and more ways to challenge the privileges of kings *and* queens.

Captivity and Conspiracy

Mary Stuart first set foot in England in the spring of 1568. Given the magnitude of the menace that she posed, Elizabeth could see few options beyond the one she chose, which was to put her cousin under lock and key. Here Mary was to remain for years while the English queen maintained the pretense that Mary was merely a guest of the crown, albeit one without liberty to refuse the company of her hosts. Permitted a substantial retinue, the cloth of the Scottish state, and most of the trappings of the queenship she had officially resigned, Mary was shuttled from English castle to English castle over the next nineteen years. She proved a dangerously charming "guest," regularly befriending her noble keepers and their wives, and all the while weaving a wide web of correspondence with all of the great rulers of Europe, including Pope Pius V and his successor, Gregory XIII.

Many of Mary's letters were written in cryptic shorthand, or "ciphers," and they often passed from (and to) the queen in secret. But she also maintained a more public correspondence, some of it with Elizabeth Tudor. Several of the letters between the two queens appear in Document 4. Poignant, querulous, and forceful by turns, Mary's messages to Elizabeth make it clear that she never recognized her long sojourn in England as less than the brutal captivity that it was. Elizabeth, for her part, was inclined to deny her own ill intentions toward Mary, and indeed she may very well have been confused about her own motives. But one thing was clear: Mary Queen of Scots compounded her own difficulties by refusing to see herself as anything other than an anointed queen, one whose crown and all of the accompanying prerogatives were still very much her own. Though she often wrote humbly to Elizabeth, Mary continued to demand that the queen declare her next in line to the English throne. And although Mary's accession would have been disastrous to a Protestant England, to cut her out of the succession would have been to admit that she had a right to it in the first place. As Elizabeth's own Parliament recognized, "this disabling shall be an enabling."[25]

At least equally disquieting were Mary's semiclandestine correspondences with the pope, with her French family and friends, and with a number of the English Catholics who supported her. Mary's letters reveal that she often knew about the rash of conspiracies always afoot against Elizabeth—particularly the Northern Rebellion of 1569 and the Ridolfi Conspiracy of 1570–71.[26] But despite the Queen of Scots's demonstrable involvement in these incidents, Elizabeth was loath to put an end to her. In part she feared retaliation by Mary's many Continental friends; equally important, she shrank from the notion of sentencing an anointed queen to death. To do so would moreover be to seek definitive resolution, and Elizabeth's style of government was based on deferral and sly equivocation. Putting an absolute end to Mary would challenge more than one foundation of Tudor authority.

The stalemate between the two queens persisted for nineteen years. In vain, Mary pleaded with Elizabeth to help restore her to her throne; she also called on her son, James, to liberate her from captivity. Now well into his teens, James had his own hopes of being named Elizabeth's successor and, valuing a political alliance with the Tudor queen above filial duty to his mother, he refused. Mary next begged Elizabeth for a personal meeting. It was not a new request: During her personal rule in Scotland,

---

[25]T. E. Hartley, ed., *Proceedings in the Parliament of Elizabeth I* (Leicester: Leicester University Press, 1981), I:374–75.

[26]During the first years of her English captivity, Mary counted on support from the earls of the north of England, particularly the powerful Lord of Northumberland. Animated partly by the possibility of Mary's marriage to the English Duke of Norfolk, some of the earls did band together against Elizabeth, but their plans were confused and incoherent. The Queen of Scots herself doubted their success, and after a short foray south, the leaders of the "Northern Rebellion" lost their resolve, disbanding before serious blood was shed. Some of them escaped to the continent, but others, including Northumberland, were beheaded. The Ridolfi Conspiracy was the inspiration of an Italian banker living in London, Roberto Ridolfi, who plotted a Spanish invasion of England to be combined with an uprising of English Catholics. Ridolfi unfortunately lacked the support of Spain itself, but he claimed to have been directly inspired by Mary (copies of her alleged instructions to him have been lost). The conspiracy was nipped in the bud, and Ridolfi's main co-conspirator, the Duke of Norfolk, was tried and executed for high treason. Analyses of the Ridolfi plot may be found in Francis Edward, *The Marvellous Chance: Thomas Howard, 4th Duke of Norfolk and the Ridolfi Plot, 1571–1572* (London: Harth Davis, 1968), and in J. H. Potter, *The English Catholics in the Reign of Elizabeth* (London: Routledge, 1920); on the Northern Rebellion, see A. Fletcher, *Tudor Rebellions* (2d ed., London: Longman's, 1973) and M. E. Jones, *Change and Continuity in the Tudor North* (York: St. Anthony's Press, 1993).

she had often wished to see Elizabeth, and in 1562 that queen had even made plans to meet with her, only to cancel them at the last minute. Now, probably frightened of her cousin's notorious personal charm and the disabling sympathy she might feel were she ever to see miserable Mary in the flesh, Elizabeth redoubled her efforts to avoid an encounter with the Queen of Scots. She succeeded: The two queens never met. Meanwhile, Mary's health collapsed. She aged rapidly, seeking refuge in her correspondence, in a menagerie of small pets, in the arts of embroidery, and, increasingly, in the Catholic religion.

Mary's Catholicism brings us to the last threat that she posed to a country increasingly dominated by Protestant tempers and interests. For one thing, her faith linked the Queen of Scots to Catholic France and papal Italy; it also put England in an awkward relation with Europe's other Catholic power, Hapsburg Spain, whose king always seemed to be searching for a reason to invade England. At the same time, England's own disaffected Catholics were naturally drawn to the Queen of Scots.[27] As the years of captivity went by, Mary herself found more and more material for the role of Catholic martyr—a role she would perfect up to the very moment of her death.

Throughout Mary Stuart's nineteen-year captivity, Elizabeth Tudor's Protestant ministers and many members of her Parliament called for the Queen of Scots to be put to death. They insisted that this "traitoress and pestilence of Christendom" was too hostile to Elizabeth to be allowed to live.[28] Others proclaimed that "Scottish Mary" had "already cost us enough of our English blood, and cares not to make havoc of nobility and people,"[29] while still others denounced her as a "bosom serpent" who, as long as England harbored her, threatened to sting the country's Protestant heart.

Anti-Catholic tensions mounted as Mary's captivity ground on. The pope excommunicated Elizabeth Tudor in 1570, and two years later the Saint Bartholomew's Day massacre of French Protestants, in which France's Catholic government was involved, made the half-French Queen of Scots less welcome in England than ever. Such incidents could only feed English Protestants' already well-nourished belief in an international

---

[27]Adrian Morley explores Roman Catholic attachment to Mary in England in *The Catholic Subjects of Elizabeth Tudor* (London: Allen & Unwin, 1978), though see Potter, *The English Catholics;* and John Bossy, "The Character of Elizabethan Catholicism," *Past and Present* 21 (1962).

[28]*CSP, Scot.,* IV:391.

[29]John Stubbes, *The Discoverie of a Gaping Gulph* (1579), in *The Gaping Gulf, with Letters and Other Relevant Documents,* ed. Lloyd E. Berry (Charlottesville, Va.: University of Virginia Press, 1968), 80.

Catholic conspiracy against them. Yet even so, Mary Stuart might have lived out her days and died a natural death had not an ardent and idealistic young English Catholic, one Anthony Babington, gotten himself arrested in the summer of 1586.

Along with several of his friends and a firebrand English priest named John Ballard, Babington was charged with conspiring to overthrow Elizabeth and replace her with the Queen of Scots. Mary had been in correspondence with Babington, and letters that had passed between them were produced. Babington confessed to Mary's role in the conspiracy and was rewarded with the standard punishment for traitors, drawing and quartering.[30] Although the letters between Mary and Babington were real, it is also likely that Elizabeth's ministers, far more eager for Mary's death than was Elizabeth herself, doctored at least one of them, adding a postscript that seemed to request the names of Babington's co-conspirators.[31] It is certain in any case that Elizabeth's ministers, led by Elizabeth's new Secretary of State, Francis Walsingham, had long monitored Mary's correspondence, regularly intercepting the letters she habitually smuggled out of her most recent and wretched prison, Chartley Castle, in a beer casket. Walsingham also secretly encouraged the Babington conspiracy, if not to frame the Queen of Scots outright, then at least with the aim of creating a situation in which she could only incriminate herself. Thanks to his efforts, Mary was confronted in early August 1586 and charged with conspiracy against the English crown. Her rooms were ransacked, and in September the Queen of Scots was removed to Fotheringay Castle, in Northamptonshire, where she would be brought to trial for treason.

The Bond of Association

The road to trial had been well paved, and not just by the tensions, contrivances, and indiscretions we have explored. Two years before Mary's trial, Elizabeth's Privy Council had drafted the so-called Bond of Association (Document 5). The Bond's chief architect was Walsingham, with

[30]Babington himself was less instrumental to the conspiracy than the militant priest, John Ballard, who seems to have preyed on the younger man's cultish devotion to Mary to realize his own political and religious vision. Close analyses of the almost laughably inept plot and Mary's involvement in it appear in Charles Nicholl, *The Reckoning: The Murder of Christopher Marlowe* (London: Jonathan Cape, 1992), and in J. H. Pollen, *Mary Queen of Scots and the Babington Plot* (Scottish History Society, third series, 1922).

[31]Walsingham's role in the apprehension of Babington and, later, Mary, is elaborated in Pollen, *Babington Plot,* and even more dramatically in Antonia Fraser's classic, *Mary Queen of Scots* (New York: Greenwich House, 1969), 475–500. See also Patrick Collinson, *The English Captivity of Mary Queen of Scots* (Sheffield: University of Sheffield Press, 1987), 6.

William Cecil (now Lord Burghley, and the queen's treasurer) also heavily involved. In essence, its effect was to license, legalize, and even organize the fate of Mary Queen of Scots. Its inspiration was ostensibly the recent discovery of yet another Catholic conspiracy against Elizabeth. A statute under Edward III had already made it high treason, punishable by death, to plot against the monarch, and this statute had often been invoked to grisly effect over the course of Elizabeth's reign, one obsessed with fears and fantasies of treason.[32]

The existence and continued applicability of the older statute notwithstanding, Elizabeth's Privy Council intended to create something new: a formal association that would include all of the "natural-born subjects of this realm of England." Mary Stuart had significant support in England, but just the same many, many thousands signed a formal "Bond" in which they vowed to do everything in their power to preserve the "great felicity" and "inestimable comfort" that Elizabeth's reign had brought them. In the wake of the fact that "the life of our gracious sovereign Queen Elizabeth hath been most dangerously designed against," the signatories—all male— swore "to prosecute, suppress and withstand all such intenders." Bound together in the "band of one firm and loyal society," they also promised to "act the utmost revenge" on anyone believed to pose a threat to Elizabeth.

The Bond of Association was essentially a lynch law, for it licensed the speediest possible punishment for an alleged crime.[33] Moreover, the Bond expanded the category of treason—invariably punishable by death—to include anyone suspected of harboring subversive thoughts against the queen, regardless of whether that person happened to be a subject of the crown. Soon the Bond of Association had passed into an official "Act for the Security of the Queen's Royal Person." The so-called Act of Association made it clear that the captive Queen of Scots was its real target, for it twice specified that "privity" to a plot against Elizabeth of "any person that shall or may pretend title to the crown of this realm" was as criminal as plotting itself. Indeed, such a person—who could only be Mary—would be "excluded and disabled for ever" from "the crown of this realm," and could even be put to death by the very subjects who had sworn to defend the reigning queen.[34]

[32]Lacey Baldwin Smith, *Treason in Tudor England: Politics and Paranoia* (Princeton: Princeton University Press, 1986).

[33]Plowden, *Two Queens*, 197. The Bond of Association and the legality of the ensuing trial are both considered in A. Francis Steuart's introduction to *The Trial of Mary Queen of Scots* (Edinburgh and London: William Hodge & Co., 1923), 9–11. Steuart reproduces several of the documents also printed in this volume.

[34]The Act of Association was followed, in 1585, by a second act—the Queen's Safety Act—which focused less on the event of an attack on Elizabeth than on the question of succession should she be killed. It barred her assailant from the throne but not his or her

The 1585 Act of Association seemed to be protecting an established monarch, Elizabeth Tudor, and, of course, fundamentally it was. But while Elizabeth—and even Mary, to show that she was harmless—had approved of it, the Act also created a way for English subjects to pressure their queen into taking action against her perceived enemies. At the same time, the Act siphoned authority from the crown by delegating the investigation and preliminary judgment of crimes against Elizabeth's "royal person" to a carefully specified commission of peers and privy counsellors. Less than two years after the Act of Association passed into law, its stipulations were to provide a perfect script for the prosecution of Mary Queen of Scots.

THE TRIAL OF MARY QUEEN OF SCOTS

An "Extraordinary Course"

Even the most casual reader of the proceedings against the Queen of Scots (Document 6) is struck by how heavily those proceedings were weighted against her. This is not just because the Act of Association had so recently made it legal to pursue those of royal blood as ruthlessly as any common subject suspected of treason. To make matters much worse, Mary herself had only a day's warning that she was actually to stand trial. A suspected rebel traitor was never allowed counsel, but the francophone Queen of Scots would be forced to conduct her own hastily cobbled defense in a language that was essentially foreign to her. Denied a single witness in her defense, Mary soon found that even her impressive familiarity with the canon law of continental Europe would be of no use to her. A treason trial was bound by English common law and statutes, and in any case the Act of Association, which legitimated the trial, was of recent vintage. Mary protested that the laws governing her trial were "by me most unknown," and so indeed they were.

In other words, Elizabeth's ministers, led by the ubiquitous and zealous Walsingham, would be hard-put to prove that they "proceed[ed] according to equity and right, and not by any cunning point of law, and extraordinary course." With considerable justification, Mary would maintain that her trial possessed nothing more substantial than the "shew and colour of just and legal proceeding." Initially she even refused to appear

---

heirs. This left the way open for Mary's Protestant son, James, to inherit the English crown, as indeed he did upon Elizabeth's death in 1603.

at it, for all that her accusers informed her that "neither her imprisonment, nor her prerogative of royal majesty could exempt her from answering in this kingdom."

From Mary's perspective, the notion of a trial was highly irregular,
indeed inappropriate, because she was an annointed queen, not a common criminal. But there is another point of view. To Mary's prosecutors
it seemed that the Queen of Scots had left her political body in Scotland
when she abdicated the throne; they had before them only Mary's natural body, stripped of its queenly might. Then too, to many of Mary's English contemporaries, her trial would have looked unusually generous, for
it did accord the queen a measure of public justice, at least on the surface. In both England and continental Europe, simple regicide was far
more common than due process of law: Indeed, three months before
Mary's trial at Fotheringay, the Prince of Orange had been murdered by
Roman Catholic assassins, and three years after it, Mary's own brother-
in-law, Henri III of France, would meet a similarly violent fate. In England, two kings (Richard II and Edward II) had been put to death without any sort of legal investigation of their alleged crimes. Some evidence
even suggests that Elizabeth would have preferred that Mary herself be
secretly poisoned without Elizabeth's official knowledge.

Mary Stuart, however, was not in the mood for gratitude. Indignant
that she was asked to "lay aside the bootless privilege of royal dignity"—
the privilege of not answering charges against her—the Queen of Scots
began to consider appearing at her own trial only when she was told that
it "could and would proceed against her, though she were absent." The
very fact that the trial "could and would" do so—that Mary's defense, like
her physical presence, was not ultimately relevant to the proceedings—
tells us how drastically the deck was stacked against her. In the end,
though, Mary's reluctant agreement to stand trial in person looks to have
been, in part, the decision of a woman anxious about her reputation. The
queen's accusers cleverly reminded her that "by avoiding Trial, you draw
upon yourself suspicion and lay upon your reputation an eternal blot and
aspersion." It was only thereafter that Mary agreed to appear in the
makeshift courtroom that had been hurriedly assembled in a room above
the great hall of Fotheringay.

When she did so appear, Mary's English prosecutors commanded virtually every detail of the scene. Thirty-six peers of the English court,
including only two Catholics, flanked the defendant (Figure 6). This
arrangement alone reminds us that Mary's trial was never a trial in the
conventional sense of a hearing before a judge and a jury of her peers.
Because Mary was a queen, she had no peer in England besides Eliza-

beth.[35] More gravely, Mary's immediate judges were the members of the commission accusing her. Her ultimate judge was to be Elizabeth Tudor herself, Mary's presumed victim. And Elizabeth was not even there; her secure absence, contrasting as it does with Mary's forced bodily presence, epitomized the Scottish queen's disadvantage. Elizabeth's person was signified "at the upper end of the chamber" by a "chair of estate," draped with a "cloth of estate" meant to represent her. Mary was assigned a humble place "below and more remote."

On this grim stage, the trial itself unfolded with sinister momentum. First, the Lord Chancellor, Sir Thomas Bromley, summarized the charges against the Queen of Scots, underscoring Elizabeth's "great grief of mind" that Mary had "conspired the Destruction of her and of England." Somewhat disingenuously, he described himself as willing to hear how Mary might "clear [herself] of [the charges] against [her], and make known [her] innocency." Next, "a historical discourse of Babington's conspiracy" was presented, one that "concluded, That [Mary] knew of it, approved it, assented unto it, promised her assistance and shewed the way and means." Babington's confession was cited, and at last the incriminating letters "betwixt her and Babington" were read out.

The first letter, from Mary to Babington, merely appointed him to deliver any correspondence that might come to the Queen of Scots from France or Scotland. But Babington's torrid reply to the woman he addressed as "my dread sovereign lady and queen, unto whom I owe all fidelity and obedience" struck a very different note. In it, he resolved to join forces with "one Ballard, a [man] of singular zeal to the Catholic cause, and your majesty's service" to accomplish "the deliverance of our country from the extreme and miserable estate wherein for a long time it hath remained." Babington promised "the hazard of my life" to serve "your sacred majesty" and assured Mary that the "chief actors" in his plot had all taken the same vow. He then described "lieutenants" posted in various parts of England and Wales, all poised to "undertake the delivery of your person from the hands of your enemies," whereupon they would embark on "the dispatch of the usurper." This last "tragical execution" would be undertaken out of "the zeal they bear to the Catholic cause, and your majesty's service." The letter concluded by asking Mary to contribute her "experience and wisdom" in order to make this scheme a reality.[36]

---

[35]Antonia Fraser makes much of this point in *Mary Queen of Scots*, 503.
[36]The letters between Babington and Mary are reproduced in full in Steuart, *Trial*, 45–51.

Mary's first response to the reading of the letter was to deny that she had ever received it. When Babington's confession was read, along with that of his cohort John Savage, averring that she had indeed received the letters, Mary insisted that the alleged reply must have been composed by her "adversaries," for it was written in secret code and not in her own hand. Nevertheless, the long reply in question was read aloud. It began by commending Babington's plan and pointing to dwindling Catholic support for the queen's cause, and it included requests for details for the planned attack on Elizabeth, culminating in "the manner of my getting forth of this hold." The letter even offered pretenses that Babington and his men might adopt in the event they were detected, and filled in many details of the plot that Babington had left vague, advocating "some stirring" in Ireland as well as in Scotland and England. The letter ended with information about when and how Babington might rescue Mary and a promise of reward.

From the first, Mary held that this was a forged letter that "proceeded not from her," and would admit to nothing more than a personal desire for liberty. Elizabeth's "destruction" could not have been further from her mind. But her denials were countered with the "Testimonies of Her Secretaries," Claude Nau and Gilbert Curle, both of whom had acknowledged her correspondence with Babington. These testimonies were, however, not actually presented to Mary "face to face," only adduced, and she was left to declare that "the majesty and safety of all princes falleth to the ground if they depend upon the Writings and Testimony of Secretaries."[37]

The first day of the trial ended in a stalemate, one that stemmed from Mary's determination to present herself as someone other than the woman that Elizabeth's commission said it was trying. To Mary's own mind she remained a foreigner and an anointed queen whose crown set her above all charges. The second day of the trial likewise began with Mary complaining that her "honour and reputation was called in question before foreign lawyers, which by wretched conclusions drew every circumstance into a consequence." She again declared herself protected by "the immunity and majesty of foreign princes," resenting that she had been "made to descend beneath her royal dignity."

With her insistence upon unassailable majesty as its foundation, Mary's defense seems to have taken most of the morning of October 16. She clearly believed that the best defense was a strong offense, for she

---

[37]Nau and Curle were actually both shown only copies of the originals, and to this extent their confession was manipulated.

hinted that Elizabeth herself had once been guilty of conspiring against Mary Tudor during her sister's reign, and she berated her own accusers for having manipulated the letters that supported the case against her. Though momentarily shaken, the English commissioners were determined, once again, to "proceed to Proofs"—something they knew Mary lacked. More letters were read, these to one of Babington's co-conspirators, and Mary again denounced her secretaries, Nau and Curle, denying as well the charge that she had planned to transfer the English crown to the Catholic king of Spain once she had gained it. The trial ended with the Queen of Scots "rising up with great confidence of countenance" to demand that she be "heard in a full Parliament, or that she might in person speak with the queen." Like every other wish she had made in the previous nineteen years, this one was not to be fulfilled, but as the queen left the room, she paused by the table where many of her prosecutors sat and hoped aloud that she would never see them again. Perhaps not dreaming to what grim letter her desire would be gratified, the Queen of Scots swept from the room.[38]

It is surprising to read of Mary Stuart's "confidence of countenance" at the end of a trial clearly tailor-made to condemn her for treason. The trial's outcome was never in question, but the defendant's apparent composure as it drew to a close reminds us of the impressive degree to which Mary was after all able to resist the barrage of evidence and accusation, at least some of it contrived, that was levelled against her. It is thus worth pausing over several features of her defense. Together these features suggest that while Mary's trial might look like little more than a legal mousetrap meant to catch the conscience of a queen, it was in reality a scene of historical transformation, one in which competing assumptions about political authority, national identity, and even the nature of femininity were forced to confront one another.

"She Was No Subject of the Queen's"

Mary's first attack on her accusers began before her trial. It was an assault on the kind of law whereby she was to be tried. Because it held even Elizabeth's equals capable of treason, we recall, this was not a law with the authority of ages behind it, but rather one that had been designed only two years before, through the Act of Association. Mary dismissed this "late law, upon which the authority of [the] Commission wholly depended," as "unjust, devised of purpose against her" and above all "without example." To this law, Mary therefore declared, "she would

---

[38]Fraser deftly captures the ironies of this moment in *Mary Queen of Scots,* 516.

never subject herself." Indeed, the only laws she could respect were either "the common law of England" — which required a precedent for a case just such as hers (there was none) — or the "canon law" of the church, in which only the upholders of that law (i.e., the pope) and not her accusers would be privileged to "interpret" the case. Though in the end she would be prosecuted by the law she scorned, Mary managed to foreground if not the outright illegality of the proceedings against her, then at least the novelty and hence the shaky authority of that law.

Mary's refusal to "subject" herself to the law points up the manmade, historically contingent nature of a legal system that presents itself as absolute; it also suggests that what actually stood trial in the fall of 1586 was the very notion of what was absolute. For Elizabeth's commissioners, the law was absolute, even though they themselves had framed it in order to defend a Protestant England that uniquely empowered them. But for Mary it was her own innate and non-negotiable sovereignty that was absolute. Her most vehement and frequent declaration was not just that she refused to be "subject" to an ill-conceived law but "that she was no subject," period: "Rather would she die a thousand deaths than acknowledge herself a subject, considering that by such an acknowledgment she should both prejudice the height of regal majesty, and withal confess herself to be bound by all the laws of England, even in matter of religion."

Valuing herself as an anointed queen, Mary exempted herself from the status of subject. And if she was not Elizabeth's subject, then by all laws other than the Act of Association, to try her for treason was illogical. For this act could only be committed by a subject, which is to say from within the political hierarchy that treason, by definition, aimed to overthrow.

Mary's claim "that she was no subject" thus damaged her prosecutors' rationale. One thing she meant by it was simply that she was "foreign." Yet to accuse Mary of treason was to assume that her place of birth, Scotland, was indeed part of England. If this was so, then why was the disowned Elizabeth on the throne and not Mary? But besides probing the sore question of what was foreign to England and what was not, Mary's insistence that she was "no subject" redounded to a much larger issue, that of the extent of a sovereign's invulnerability. This was a point of controversy that would only escalate over the next century; the English Civil Wars of the 1640s would eventually make it their main theme. But in 1586, Mary Stuart merely maintained that "justice" would be served only when her accusers realized that, as an annointed queen, she stood above all earthly law.

Their notion of justice was very different: As one of the commissioners, the Vice Chamberlain Sir Christopher Hatton, pointed out, from the

English point of view "all justice would stagger, yea, fall to the ground" if "the royal dignity" was to be exempted from the charge of such a crime. Mary's unsupported claims of sovereignty's immunity from the laws that rule the ordinary human would remind us, then, that like that of what was and was not England (or English) an integrated concept of justice had split open at the seams.

Mary's distinction between what lay above the law and what lay below it resonated in a different key as well, for another of her defenses was to remind the Commission that what was happening in their makeshift court was not a matter limited to England, or even to the petty domain of terrestrial political concerns: Even before the trial began, Mary insisted that her trial unfolded on a higher, and fundamentally moral, stage—in "the theatre of the whole world," which was "much wider than the kingdom of England," and whose audience, she implied, was finally God. Throughout her trial, Mary "appealed to [the] consciences" of her adversaries, and denied that she would ever "make shipwreck of my soul by conspiring the destruction of my dearest sister." Toward the end of the trial, Mary identified herself with the virtuous queens of the Old Testament, declaring that "she had rather play Hester than Judith; make intercession to God for the people than deprive the meanest of people of life." She even presented the execution of Babington as the death of a Catholic martyr to her own cause, provoking both the Lord Treasurer and Walsingham himself to an indignant defense that temporarily turned the tables, forcing them to explain themselves almost as fully as Mary had thus far been compelled to account for herself.

Mary also seems to have conceived of her trial as part of a larger *imitatio Christi*—the symbolic process, cultivated in medieval times, whereby human beings molded their own miseries to resemble the redemptive suffering of Christ. After her trial, the Queen of Scots would complain that she had been treated as Christ had at the end of his life, and it is worth noting that he too had been tried and crucified because he had treasonously proclaimed himself a sovereign, in his case King of the Jews. Whether or not Mary was interested in the full scope of the analogy between her situation and Christ's, it is clear that she did everything in her power to give her trial the form and meaning of religious experience.

By shifting her trial to a spiritual stage, Mary Stuart stood a chance of winning even despite earthly defeat.[39] Her manner of self-presentation

---

[39]This was a strategy that Mary's grandson, Charles I, would exploit when he was tried by his own subjects in 1649. See Daniel P. Klein, "The Trial of Charles I," *Legal History* 18 (1997): 1–25.

was highly theatrical and transformed the proceedings against her from a fixed tableau of immutable guilt into a scene of volatile debate. Mary's determination to make her trial as dramatic and unpredictable as possible brings us to a final conflict whose repercussions were to vibrate far beyond Fotheringay in space and time. We recall that the Stuart queen's favorite strategy of resistance was to deny that she had written the letters in question: "With a countenance composed to royal dignity and with a mind untroubled" she disavowed all connection with the "word and writing" that had been produced against her. In point of fact, the charges against Mary depended very heavily upon the written word's authority to compel belief in guilt or innocence. But the Queen of Scots strove to call writing's very authority into question, not only by denying that the letters could count as proof positive, but even by disdaining to give her accusers any written version of her response to Elizabeth's "scruples." Instead, she spoke without notes—"for it stood not, said she, with her royal dignity, to play the scrivener."

From the beginning of the trial to its end, Mary based her defense on hostility to the abstract impersonality of the written word—symbols detached, she implied, from the physical and even moral realities of her situation. This strategy has roots in religious ideology, for since its inception earlier in the century, the Protestant faith had built itself on the written words of holy scripture, in defiance of the icons and rituals that were the cornerstone of Roman Catholic religious practice. Especially in contrast to that of the Roman Catholic Church, Protestant authority tended to rest upon the abstractions of the written word, and this was precisely where the legal attack on Mary Stuart had its roots, too.

But the Queen of Scots insisted on an altogether different system of meaning, one grounded less in language than in the human body. Her words were often eloquent, too, but Mary foremost made her physical frame, crippled by nearly two decades of confinement, a moving object for all to see. In essence, she presented her body as evidence to counter that supplied by writing. By challenging writing's authority and redirecting attention to her own flesh, Mary refuted the Protestant assumptions that were the underpinnings of her trial. To this effect she repeatedly interrupted the reading of the letters, and "fell into speeches" again and again. She "wandered far in these digressions" and, "called back again and prayed . . . to speak plainly," she was more likely to weep. "Tears burst forth from her incessantly," we are told. "Withal she shed plenty of tears."

Mary Stuart's tears produced several effects. For one thing, they complemented the queen's insistence that other laws and rules could be applied to the situation at hand. If her trial were to end as Elizabeth's commissioners so visibly wished it to end, this wouldn't be because right had prevailed. Rather, it would be because one (visibly manufactured) set of legal conventions, political assumptions, and standards of evidence had defeated another, more archaic paradigm of truth based on blood right and pity for the plight of another. Furthermore, the bodies of condemned criminals were traditionally meaningful symbols of their guilt: In London, heads were impaled on Tower Bridge to make an example of their former owners, and Mary's own supposed accomplice, Anthony Babington, had like many another traitor been drawn and quartered because that bloody spectacle would serve as a warning and reinforce the impression of his guilt.

Frequently, felons and traitors even cooperated in their own physical degradation. But Mary refused to play the game. Through her tears and the pathetic display of her suffering body, she aimed not to confirm her own guilt but rather to disrupt the charges against her, antagonizing the very legal system into which her body was supposed to fit. She would later employ the same strategy at her execution, presenting herself there not as a repentant enemy of the state but rather as a suffering martyr for her faith.

Finally, in weeping, Mary drew upon an obviously gendered form of expression. While in her day tears were less likely to be considered the sole provenance of women than they are now, "womanly weeping" remained a very particular phenomenon; many onlookers would have remembered, for example, that at Christ's crucifixion it was women who wept (Luke 2:28). Just so, Mary's frequent tears and displays of emotion encouraged her accusers to see her as a woman, and especially as a woman in distress. The white veil of mourning that she wore was also bound to attract sympathy, helping the Queen of Scots to exploit a specifically feminine aura of vulnerability.[40] We've already seen that she also aligned herself with the biblical heroine Esther, famed for her feminine mildness.

Mary Stuart's inventive defense was not enough to change the scheduled outcome of her trial. But both her surprising eloquence and her tactics of disruptive resistance allow the trial record as we have it to provoke multiple interpretations, responses, and feelings. By shifting the platform of her own authority and by challenging the one that her accusers had built for the occasion, Mary paved the way to future, strikingly

---

[40]The veil, or one reputed to be it, is now on display at London's Victoria and Albert Museum.

ambivalent, imaginative treatments of the trial like the one that we find in the court poet Edmund Spenser's allegory, *The Faerie Queene* (1590–96).

Of course, Mary's defense only made a symbolic difference. It did not alter the legal outcome of her trial. The only question that really remained was that of how the Queen of Scots's guilt would be used and interpreted. And as it happened, immediate judgment was delayed—not because of anything the defendant was able to say or do, but rather because Elizabeth called the commissioners back to London before they could announce their verdict. In any case, it was Elizabeth who had finally to decide what Mary's punishment should be. That meant, ironically enough, that it was the very queen supposedly in danger who kept it possible that anything at all might have happened next.

"Answers Answerless": Elizabeth's Struggles with Parliament

An enormous and vociferous proportion of the members of Elizabeth's Parliament had long wanted Mary Stuart dead. After her trial, their voices were joined by those of other, less illustrious English subjects, many of whom published impassioned arguments for the "Necessity of the Sentence of Death." The author of one such treatise typically held that, had she not been caught, the Queen of Scots would have "spared no device or unmerciful feat to have accomplished her will, in revenge of her imprisonment." To his mind, Mary desired nothing less than the "persecution of the Protestants" and the "transformation of the laws, rights and usages of the realm to the appetite of strangers."[41] Such accusations suggest that expelling Mary was less about protecting Elizabeth (the premise of the Act of Association) than it was about purifying "the realm" of England from the contamination of "strangers," especially non-Protestant ones. Those in favor of Mary's expulsion were tormented by the thought of the French or even Spanish Catholic government she might bring in were she ever to take Elizabeth's place; they dreaded domination by "partial and evil affected Aliens."[42]

It was, however, for Elizabeth, not them, to decide what ought to be done about Mary. It was Elizabeth who could pardon her, and if a sentence of death were to be issued, it was Elizabeth who would have to issue it. Hence petition after petition made its way to the Tudor queen, each presenting the Queen of Scots as the root of all evil, author of the many

---

[41] "Necessity of the Sentence of Death" (1586), *CSP, Scot.*, IX:384.
[42] *A Defence of the Execution of Mary Queen of Scots* (1586), F3r.

rifts and schisms dividing a country that, they implied, would otherwise have enjoyed a happy unity. At the same time, the heated rhetoric that called for Mary's head also raised one of the most troublesome ghosts of her reign—the ever-shaky status of female monarchy. One analysis of Mary's "horrible and unnatural attempts and actions," for example, maintained that though the two queens were "of like sex and quality," Elizabeth owed Mary no womanly pity, for "what compassion is to be had of her who has transgressed the bounds of that modesty and meekness that her sex and quality prescribes?"[43]

On the surface, charging Mary with a crime against virtuous womanhood was meant to absolve Elizabeth herself of the necessity of behaving compassionately, as otherwise a woman should: If Mary had "transgressed the bounds" of prescribed feminine "modesty and meekness," then Elizabeth would be justified in doing the same, and seeking her blood. But such formulations were dangerous, for they invariably recalled the fact that the two queens were "of like sex and quality" and that aspersions cast upon Mary were all too likely to reflect upon Elizabeth as well.

No matter how Elizabeth responded to Mary's trial, she would thus be drawing attention to the deepest uncertainties of her reign. Indeed, the very fact that Mary was on trial for treason would have brought to mind Knox's assertion in his *First Blast of the Trumpet* that the woman who "reigneth above man" did so only through "treason and conspiracy committed against God." If female rule was itself treason, then Elizabeth, in putting Mary to death for treason, might be in some way condemning herself as well. At the very least, she ran the risk of appearing as much a criminal against female virtue as Mary herself had seemed. Yet in letting Mary live, Elizabeth would be subordinating her most powerful subjects' wills to her own—an act of doubtful integrity on the part of either a lovable monarch or a virtuous woman.

The dilemma that confronted the Tudor queen as her Parliament pressed her to put an end to Mary's life cannot be underestimated. Elizabeth knew that to sentence Mary to death would be to blot her own name, as both a monarch and a woman. And she knew that it would also be to bring down the wrath of Valois and Hapsburg Europe alike, as well as to alienate Elizabeth's own Catholic subjects. Understandably the English queen's response to the Mary Stuart problem was thus to temporize. Nor is it surprising that her desire to postpone a decision should have pitted an ambivalent Elizabeth against a male Parliament's single-minded quest for her rival's death. Elizabeth's words on the subject therefore

---

[43]"The Policy and Justice of the Proposed Execution of Mary" (1586), *CSP, Scot.*, IX:251.

chart a kind of verbal isthmus between Parliament's unequivocal clamorings and Mary's own relatively straightforward strategies of defense.

To appreciate Elizabeth's struggle with Parliament in the last months of Mary Stuart's life, we need to consider what her relationship to that body had been like before. We saw that in the reign of Henry VIII, the crown had grown increasingly dependent on Parliament, especially for tax revenues. Although Elizabeth inherited this dependence, and also had to call on Parliament to settle numerous matters of legislation and policy, she had always, by and large, held her own, and seen her will done as a result. When there was disagreement with the queen, Parliament's two houses were seldom sufficiently unified to oppose her, and in any case Elizabeth's superior power, as monarch, was generally respected. It is true that the first decades of Elizabeth's reign had seen conflicts over such issues as religion and the Tudor queen's possible marriage, and that Elizabeth was much more conservative than Parliament as a whole, almost always less inclined to take rapid action in both foreign and domestic affairs. Potential crises were usually resolved to Elizabeth's satisfaction because she was extraordinarily agile politically, and made sure to involve herself in parliamentary sessions, appearing always at their opening and closing, and often cleverly playing the members of both houses against one another.

Against the background of this tradition, the Mary Queen of Scots affair stands out sharply. A unified Parliament was thirsty for Mary's blood, a suddenly isolated Elizabeth reluctant to shed it. The queen thus kept uncharacteristically aloof from the parliamentary sessions that took place in the wake of Mary's trial, and when she did address Parliament, she did so in the form of two long and painstakingly crafted speeches (Document 7). Both speeches responded to official calls for Mary's death — calls that aimed to paint Elizabeth into a political corner, leaving her no choice but to have Mary's head.

On October 25, nine days after the conclusion of Mary's trial, the conciliar court, known as the Star Chamber and consisting of Elizabeth's Privy Council and certain judges, had met at Westminster, and declared definitively that Mary Stuart had "compassed and imagined within this realm of England, divers matters tending to the hurt, death, and destruction" of Elizabeth. After this preliminary judgment had been passed, Parliament erupted into several days of impassioned speechifying against the scarlet "Jezebel," Mary Queen of Scots. Mary was denounced as "the daughter of sedition, the mother of rebellion, the nurse of impiety, the handmaid of iniquity, the sister of unshamefastness."[44] Again and again,

---

[44]Job Throckmorton, in Neale, *Parliaments*, II:11.

the Queen of Scots's sex colored all of the crimes of which she stood accused, be they sedition, rebellion, or even simple shamelessness. Bitter misogyny both magnified English hatred of Mary and provided an inflammatory vocabulary for widespread fear and loathing of Catholic and Continental domination.

Before long, both houses of Parliament addressed a joint "supplication" to Elizabeth, holding up to her the "most dangerous and execrable practices" of the Queen of Scots. That queen, it was declared, had designed first "to ruinate and overthrow the happy State and Commonweal of this most noble realm" and then "to bereave us of the sincere and true Religion of Almighty God, bringing us and this noble crown back again into the thraldom of the Romish tyranny." Parliament praised Elizabeth for having shown extraordinary clemency to Mary in the past. But, they warned, an "insolent boldness is grown in the heart of the same queen": "If the said lady should now escape the due and deserved punishment of Death, for these her most execrable Treasons and Offences, your highness's royal person shall be exposed unto many more." They thus urged Elizabeth "to take speedy order" and seek "the just and speedy execution of the said Queen." Not to do so would "procure the heavy displeasure and punishment of Almighty God." At the very least, "the effect and true meaning" of the recent Act of Association demanded Mary's death.[45]

As Parliament created an atmosphere of haste and urgency and invoked the wrath of God in tandem with the earthly directives of the Act of Association, its members seemed to have sought dominion over their queen. But the matter is more complicated. As one historian has demonstrated, Elizabeth herself evidently asked the authors of the petition to insert their seemingly coercive reference to the Act of Association because it relieved her of some of the burden of decision.[46] Most recent analysts of Elizabeth's speeches even surmise that she would have been happiest had her Parliament taken Mary's punishment into their own hands. We might in any event say that the Mary Stuart problem struck at Elizabeth's queenly authority in a complicated way — not just by subjecting the queen's will to that of Parliament but, more subtly, by forcing her to *want* to divest herself of a royal prerogative that she, not unlike Mary, held dear.

Elizabeth's first speech to Parliament was thus designed to stall for time. When she finally delivered it, it turned out to be a masterpiece of sinuous equivocation, one that could not have differed more dramatically from Mary's fundamentally unwavering (if tearful) defense at her trial.

---

[45]Parliament's first petition to Elizabeth is reproduced in Steuart, *Trial*, 62–64.
[46]Neale, *Parliaments*, II:115.

Both queens confronted a unified group of male subjects who demanded a single and definite resolution to a longstanding complexity. Unlike Mary's defiant insistence on her own unassailable majesty, however, Elizabeth's first speech to Parliament began with expressions of deepest humility. At first, this humility was directed to a God who had so often and so "miraculously preserved" Elizabeth from harm. But gradually it was transformed into gratitude to the "good wills" of her own subjects. The sorrowful, oddly intimate language of self-reflection that permeated her speech likewise submitted Elizabeth's very heart to her listeners, meekly acknowledging her dependence on them.

Like Mary's, Elizabeth's words functioned partly as a defense: The Tudor queen defended herself from the need to make a decision about Mary, but she also defended the law whereby Mary herself was tried. This double allegiance—to another queen and to her people—structures Elizabeth's speech. And indeed she proved nimble at playing both of her own affiliations against one another, evidently to buy more time for herself. Elizabeth herself declared that she and Mary were "not different in sex, of like estate"—such "near kin" that, had the two queens been "but as milk-maids, with pails upon our arms," Elizabeth could never have been induced to harm her cousin.

Of course, Elizabeth realized that she and Mary were very far from milkmaids, but this too becomes a point of kinship. Elizabeth emphasized that the Queen of Scots was not tried by jury precisely because she was a queen—"a proper course forsooth if trial against a Princess!" Indeed, even more than royal blood, Elizabeth and Mary seemed to share the vulnerability of kings, and it is this vulnerability, not royal power, that Elizabeth attempted to use as well as acknowledge, noting that "we princes are set as it were upon stages, in the sight and view of all the world. The least spot is soon spied in our garments, a blemish quickly noted in our doings" (Document 7).

Even as it expresses sympathy with Mary, however, Elizabeth's first parliamentary speech stresses her allegiance to her own subjects, beginning with her dependence on their "good wills" and drawing to a close by invoking the Act of Association, "which as I do acknowledge as a strong argument of your true hearts, and great zeal to my safety, so shall my bond be stronger tied to a greater care for all your good." The bond with her people that was sealed by the Act of Association is pitted against her blood bond with the Queen of Scots; identification with another woman (and cousin) competes with gratitude to a relatively abstract corporation of male subjects. In her speech, Elizabeth refused to choose between these bonds. And as long as she held on to both of them, she could avoid "present resolution." Her first address to Parliament thus ends with the inconclusive promise "to deliberate long upon that which is once to be resolved."

We should beware of seeing Elizabeth's circular, slippery, indefinite speech as simply the utterance of her true feelings, a guileless expression of her psychological conflict as she debated killing someone she saw as more like herself than otherwise. It was also a rhetorical form, designed if not to persuade its audience, then at least to buy time from it. And it succeeded in part because Elizabeth was willing to play a stereotypical female role before her audience, appearing to submit to them as a woman should.

Elizabeth's first speech to Parliament may also be seen as a dramatization of England's own struggle to determine what was like and unlike itself. Parliament demanded that that struggle be resolved. It responded immediately to Elizabeth, in a strident and unyielding voice that contrasts dramatically with the queen's evasive words. Voiced by the speaker of the House of Commons, Sir John Puckering (or Pikeryng), Parliament's second plea for Elizabeth to put her "impatient Competitor" out of her misery was based on the idea that "the welfare and the hurt of the prince belongeth to all." If the sovereign fundamentally "belongeth" to her subjects, Puckering maintained, then this belonging takes precedence over any loyalty she might have to another ruler. "To spare her is to spill us," Puckering insisted, whereas Mary "is only a cousin to you in a remote degree."

Puckering's reasoning proceeded logically, even moving from numbered point to numbered point as he warned that Elizabeth could never be safe while Mary lived, nor could "religion" be, let alone England's "present state" of peace and unity. Despite its rational structure, however, the real force of Puckering's speech lay in its thinly veiled threat to Elizabeth, for he warned that in the end she would "deservedly provoke the heavy hand and wrath of God" should she fail to strike Mary down. The threat returned when Puckering hinted that the Act of Association licensed Elizabeth's subjects to take Mary's life "without direction," and that Elizabeth herself was bound by that same law: To let Mary live would be to defy it.

At the same time, Puckering carefully tailored his petition to Elizabeth's sex, all the while invoking Mary's, for his favorite metaphor was one that cast the people of England as Elizabeth's children. Here again the question of how closely Elizabeth was actually related to Mary—and what she therefore owed her—came into play, for Puckering held that while Mary was only a remote cousin, "we be the sons and children of this land, whereof you be not only the natural mother, but also the wedded spouse." This being so, "it would exceedingly grieve and wound the hearts of your loving subjects" to allow Mary to live.[47]

In his rejoinder to Elizabeth's first speech, Puckering in effect asserted two bonds between the people of England and their female ruler, both meant less to empower Elizabeth than to manipulate her. One was the bond of romantic love, in which to spare Mary would be to "wound" England's heart. The other, more potent, bond was a maternal one, which any mercy for Mary would sever: "If she prevail, she will rather make us slaves, than take us for her children; and therefore the realm sigheth and groaneth under fear of such a step-mother." Just as Mary the traitor was supposed to have violated the boundaries of proper femininity, so did Mary, England's potential queen, desecrate another appropriate female role—one that Elizabeth embodied, for "with more than motherly piety you have always cherished us the children of the land." In turn, by allowing Mary to live, Elizabeth would become a bad mother to her children-people.

Powerful as these arguments and images might be, however, the most thunderous resonance of Puckering's speech came from its invocation of the Protestant state. That state, Puckering held, would end as Mary's Catholic state began, for she had been "poisoned with popery from her tender youth" and was "so devoted and doted" to "popery" that she could only be expected to "supplant the gospel where and whensoever she may." Puckering enjoined Elizabeth to follow the biblical precedent in which "those mischievous and wicked queens, Jezebel and Athalia" were direly punished, and in his speech the diverse languages of love, nature, and faith all converged to create the impression of "one voice and mind making humble and instant suit" that Mary Queen of Scots must die . . . and Elizabeth Queen of England yield to the will of her people. That the two queens thus appear to share the same situation gave eerie force to the inversions that filled Puckering's speech and bound the two women together in other ways: "As her life threatened your death, so her death may, by God's favour, prolong your life," Puckering prophesied. "Mercy in this case will in the end prove cruelty against all."[48]

Clearly Elizabeth must respond. But how? Though much briefer than her earlier speech, the queen's second address to Parliament was even more contorted and elusive than the first had been. Indeed, William

---

[47] Puckering's metaphor was not uncommon. An anonymous pamphlet of the day accused Mary of inciting Elizabeth's subjects to "gnaw the womb of our common mother." See *A Defence of the Execution of Mary Queen of Scots* (1586), 40.
[48] Puckering's speech is reproduced in Steuart, *Trial*, 67–71.

Warner, author of the Elizabethan chronicle *Albions England,* compared the queen's address to "King Gordian's Knot," for the speech was so grammatically intricate, its logic so densely interwoven, and its syntax so convoluted, that its audience was hard-put to penetrate its true meaning. Was Elizabeth indirectly asking—as to many she seemed to be—that "some other means" than public execution be used "to work my safety"? Or was this what she herself pronounced it at the end, a helpless "answer-answerless" to the question of whether Mary Stuart should be sentenced to death?

The individual reader must make up his or her own mind as to what Elizabeth meant by her "answer-answerless." Nonetheless, it is possible to consider some of the rhetorical strands of Elizabeth's oration. First, and most noticeably, there is simply its style. Elizabeth's sentences are all clogged with qualifying phrases and subordinate clauses piled one on top of the other. The speech boasts many of the *topoi,* or common-places, of classical rhetoric—examples of past rulers confronted with agonizing decisions, allusions to the difficulty of speaking, a list of self-congratulations that the speaker pretends *not* to give. But none of these *topoi* is pursued for very long, and instead of supplying the speech with a venerable and confident infrastructure, they only thicken its patina of indecision.

The speech is also fraught with Elizabeth's consciousness of her own womanhood. She plays with the image of her Parliament as "suitors" and of herself as someone driven by "greedy desire." The erotic language that runs through the speech keeps the sex of the speaker in the foreground, and Elizabeth had always been famous for her ability to employ this technique with playful agility. But in this case, Elizabeth's efforts to eroticize her relationship to her male listeners falls flat, and is indeed often buried under the more burdensome aspects of respectable femininity, especially a woman's dependence for authority upon her own good name. Thus Elizabeth wonders "what is it which they not write now, when they shall hear that I have given consent, that the executioner's hands shall be imbued with the blood of my nearest kinswoman?"

As if to resolve a dilemma compounded by her own sex, Elizabeth takes a tack reminiscent of the one Mary used when she invoked the heroines of the Old Testament, Esther and Judith. But instead of women of scripture, the English queen aligns herself with the ancient Greek leader Alcibiades, also lacing her speech with structural allusions to the wise king Solomon. In essence, her speech takes flight from the imagery of queenship altogether: only men can hope for the aura of invulnerability that Elizabeth seeks.

Accordingly, Elizabeth's speech foregrounds mental (typically male), not emotional (typically female), activity: The inward processes of "judgment" and "knowledge" become its theme. Elizabeth even lapses into a long and seemingly unmotivated account of her life, beginning with the days "when first I took the sceptre" and emphasizing both the "perils" of that time and her own habits of lengthy and rational deliberation. The point of this self-reflective digression may be similar to the point of Mary's efforts to establish her foreignness and inalienable majesty: Each queen fought to define who and what she was.

But the most conspicuous feature of Elizabeth's speech is its failure to resolve the situation at hand. The address to Parliament begins and ends with the same sort of paradox: First the queen places herself between two incompatible linguistic possibilities—"whether I should speak or use silence." Similarly, she ends by classifying what she has spoken as an "answer-answerless." While this inconclusiveness might be seen as a deferral strategy, we could also understand it as a function of Elizabeth's queenly predicament—the fact that no legal or official vocabulary existed to communicate the difficult situation at hand.

Elizabeth's two speeches were not only intended for the ears of Parliament; they were also meant for the eyes of her people, and she diligently polished them before Francis Walsingham had them printed, both in the vernacular and in Latin translation. Walsingham also published Parliament's petitions for the sentence of death to be passed against Mary, thereby creating the politically useful image of a queen under pressure from her subjects. Elizabeth herself participated in the creation of that image, whose purpose was, in the end, to absolve her of full guilt in Mary's death. On the surface, that is, the queen's exchanges with Parliament look like evidence of her submission to her own subjects. But this surface impression may well have been one that Elizabeth wished to exploit, a means whereby she actually attempted to protect her own authority, especially to the extent that that authority required that she be judged a just queen and a woman of flawless repute.

At first glance, Elizabeth's speeches seem only to contrast dramatically with Mary's defense at her trial, the most striking difference lying in the way that the two queens presented themselves to their audiences. Mary, we recall, insisted unequivocally upon her own "regal majesty," and from its height eschewed all deference to English law. Elizabeth, by contrast, fully acknowledged that she was trapped, declaring that "by this last Act of Parliament you have brought me to a narrow streight, that I must give order for her death, which is a princess most nearly allied unto me in blood." Yet both queens were ultimately vulnerable to the will of Parliament. Elizabeth had a history of managing to see her own will done, the far less strategic Mary a history of succumbing to the will of others. Elizabeth's speeches reveal that in this instance her own will could not be done, partly because it could not be known entirely even to herself.

There were in any event numerous pragmatic reasons for Elizabeth to delay decision as long as possible. Besides not wanting to have Mary's blood on her hands, Elizabeth feared Scottish and French retaliation. At least equally important, Mary's life had become a guarantee that Philip of Spain would not attempt to invade England. Yet popular anxiety was building. War with Spain had broken out in 1585, fueling popular hysteria about a possible Hapsburg invasion, regardless of the Queen of Scots's fate. That wild fear combined with poor economic conditions and rising prices to create an atmosphere of extreme domestic disquiet, one Mary Stuart's presence only seemed to exacerbate. Thus in early December, Elizabeth apparently made up her mind, and on December 4 she proclaimed the sentence of Mary's death. Almost at once ambassadors from Scotland and France began to arrive in order to bargain for the Queen of Scots's life.

Mary's own reaction to the sentence of death was somewhat different. She expressed it in her last letter to Elizabeth (Document 4). Signed "your sister and cousin wrongfully imprisoned, Marie, Queen," the letter does not protest against its author's fate. Rather, Mary presents herself as a martyr to the Catholic faith and requests burial in France alongside her mother, Marie de Guise. Her most poignant plea, however, is for Elizabeth "not to permit that my execution take place without your knowledge; not for fear of the torment, which I am very ready to suffer, but for the rumours that would be spread about my death, without witnesses."

What sort of "rumours" might possibly be spread about Mary's death? Mary's concern about them reprises a leitmotiv in the story of her trial and its aftermath. We have seen how much this historical episode revolved around matters of fiction and representation: Mary's enemies — Elizabeth's ministers — had built a trap for her, probably tampered with the evidence against her, and manipulated the Queen of Scots by preying upon her fears that her reputation would be ruined if she refused to appear in a carefully contrived court authorized by a recently invented law. Elizabeth's second speech to Parliament in particular had betrayed her painful consciousness that it was crucial, if almost impossible, to control the way that she was seen by others. She noted the "many defamatory Books and Pamphlets against me, accusing me to be a tyrant" and dreaded what would be said against her when it "shall be spread" that

"a maiden queen" had "spilled the blood even of her own kinswoman."
Mary's fear of "rumour" was thus well-founded. And her English enemies shared her desire to control the way in which the end of her life
was to be interpreted, fearful lest the Queen of Scots be construed as
something far more heroic than a dire and scandalous enemy to the English state.

In the end, Mary's execution, on February 8, 1587, turned out to justify fears that its meaning could not be regulated. But it is only by turning, at last, to contemporary treatments of the execution itself that we can
see how fully those fears were justified: The social, political, psychological, and moral dilemmas that the treason trial had laid open were by no
means resolved by Mary's death, but in fact lived on through it.

"In My End Is My Beginning": The Death of Mary Stuart

Although Elizabeth proclaimed the sentence of death in early December,
Mary's execution itself was delayed. December and January went by,
bringing, in Walsingham's words, "false bruits . . . that the Queen of Scots
was broken out of prison, that the city of London was fired; that many
thousand Spaniards were landed in Wales."[49] In the frantic atmosphere
that these rumors created, Elizabeth at last signed Mary's death warrant,
consulting anxiously with her ministers over its wording. During this
time, Elizabeth's Secretary of State Francis Walsingham—Mary's most
formidable and persistent enemy heretofore—fell ill and was replaced
by one William Davison. Many suspected Walsingham's sickness was a
political ploy, devised at the last minute to avoid direct responsibility for
Mary's death. In any case, it was under Davison's direction that the warrant, accompanied by formal letters from the Tudor queen's council, was
sent to Fotheringay Castle.

Once Elizabeth learned that the death warrant had been dispatched,
she was furious, declaring that Davison had acted without consulting
her. As if to shift the burden of responsibility, Elizabeth even slyly
reported a dream in which Mary's death had driven her to rage. But the
queen could rant and rave all she liked: The warrant was already on its
way to Fotheringay, and there it was immediately put into effect by Sir
Amyas Paulet, Mary's grim and rigorous Puritan keeper. Under Paulet's
direction, a scaffold was erected in the great hall of Fotheringay. With
the sound of the hammer ringing in her ears, Mary set about making

---

[49]Conyers Read, *Mr. Secretary Walsingham and the Policy of Queen Elizabeth* (Oxford:
Oxford University Press, 1925), III:60–62.

her own final arrangements: She was determined to turn her execution into a stage for her vindication as a martyr to the Roman Catholic Church, and thus as the foundation of her symbolic victory over Elizabeth of England. Certainly, the situation was tailor-made to inspire sympathy for the Queen of Scots. She arrived at her own beheading splendidly dressed, serenely enjoining her devoted women in waiting not to weep, forgiving her executioners, murmuring psalms in Latin, and commanding the scene to the end.

But what *was* the end of the scene? Throughout Mary's captivity, a cryptic motto embroidered in cloth had hung above her chair of state: "En ma fin est mon commencement" ("in my end is my beginning"). These words proved prescient, for in an important sense the end of Mary's mortal life marked the beginning of a tide of controversial writings and new images of the queen that would flow for centuries. The vast difference between two contemporary accounts of the execution—one by an eyewitness, Robert Wyngfield, and one by a Scottish Catholic living in France, Adam Blackwood—dramatizes the extent to which an event intended to achieve resolution merely perpetuated conflict and controversy.

The Protestant Wyngfield's *Circumstantial Account of the Execution of Mary, Queen of Scots* (Document 8) tells us much about how Mary's enemies saw her in the end. As she approached the scaffold, Wyngfield reports, the queen was

> of stature tall, of body corpulent, round-shouldered, her face fat and broad, double-chinned, and hazel-eyed, with borrowed hair. . . . Her attire was this: On her head she had a dressing of lawn, edged with bone lace, a pomander chain and an *Agnus Dei* about her neck, a crucifix in her hand, a pair of beads in her girdle, with a golden cross at the end of them, a veil of lawn fastened to her caul, bowed out with wire, and edged round about with bone-lace . . . her sleeves to the ground, with acorn buttons of jet, trimmed with pearl, . . . her girdle whole, of figured black satin, and her petticoat skirts of crimson velvet.

Wyngfield treated his Elizabethan readers to an even gaudier inventory of Mary's girdle and petticoat, her "shoes of Spanish leather," her green silk garters, and silver-clocked hose. Then, by his report, Mary began to divest herself of her rosary and crucifix, handing them to her distraught female attendants. "She made herself unready with a kind of gladness," Wyngfield conceded, and throughout her disrobing "never altered her countenance" but instead, "smiling, said, to the executioners, she never had such grooms before to make her unready, nor ever put off her clothes before such company." This flirtatious Mary then crossed herself, kneeled, and without any token of the fear of death, said [a psalm in Latin] ... Then, groping for the block, she laid down her head, putting her chain over her back with both her hands.... Then she laid herself upon the block most quietly, and stretching out her arms and legs cried out ["In your hands, God, I commend my spirit"], three or four times. At last whilst one of the executioners held her straightly with one of his hands, the other gave two strokes with an axe before he did cut off her head, and yet left a little gristle behind.

Colorful, grotesque, yet tinged with erotic nuance, Wyngfield's account converts Mary into a carnival attraction. The brilliant costume, the repeated smiles, the jokes, wig, and "corpulent," inflated, and ungainly body all suggest a clown more than a woman. Such details conspire to strip the Queen of Scots of all suggestion that she might be a Catholic martyr. In this light, the most vivid detail of Wyngfield's account comes when the executioner holds her head aloft. For at that moment, Wyngfield testifies, the queen's artfully woven hairpiece slipped aside to reveal that the youthful, almost vibrant beauty who had spoken her last words only moments before was in reality a gray and ailing woman, no longer recognizable, "her face much altered" and her lips grotesquely stirring "up and down almost a quarter of an hour after her head was cut off."

Such macabre (and often apocryphal) details remind us that Wyngfield wrote from the perspective of one who wanted Mary Stuart dead. Although it is surprisingly objective, and even touching in many ways, his description of the execution also aims to erase the queen from the scene of her death, seizing control of the image she had fought to design and regulate. Later the same year, however, a very different version of the execution, excerpted in Document 9, was published in Paris. Eventually translated into English as *The History of Mary Queen of Scots,* Adam Blackwood's *Martyre de la royne d'Escosse* cast the Queen of Scots as a martyr to English Protestant barbarity in general and to her "cruel cousin Elizabeth" in particular. It is to some extent the literary equivalent of the portrait of Mary as a Catholic heroine (Figure 7) that was made shortly after her death. Coming, logically, at the end of a hagiographic treatment of Mary's life, Blackwood's account presents Mary's bodily decrepitude as the result of her harsh confinement. It also magnifies her "true piety." On the way to the scaffold, for instance, the queen points out that the cross she carries corresponds to her heartfelt reflection on Christ's death—a death that hers is clearly meant to imitate.

Whereas Wyngfield inflates many details of Mary's physical appearance until she resembles nothing so much as a garish *grande dame,* Blackwood invokes a moral and spiritual framework to give the execution a specific meaning within the martyrological tradition. Wyngfield's grimly factual language contrasts with Blackwood's insertion of damning adjectives and vivid figures of speech, apparent, for example, when he describes the "shameless executioner" and speaks of "the butcher's hands." And where Wyngfield ruthlessly itemizes Mary's own body, Blackwood contextualizes her execution within the responses of her sympathetic audience. He marks the "watery eyes and sorrowful hearts" of her women in waiting and declares that even "her hardest-hearted enemies were greatly moved": "There was only two or three persons that could withhold weeping."

In turn, for Blackwood, the actions of the executioner amount to the brutal ravishment of a defenseless woman: Mary's gown is "stripped down to the middle" and she is "snatched . . . rudely by the arms," stripped of her doublet and bodice, "so that her neck being all naked appeared to the spectators more white than snow or alabaster." Unlike Wyngfield, Blackwood allows Mary herself to speak at great length, showering blessings and prayers all around while the Dean of Peterborough does all he can "to interrupt her." Interested in arousing Catholic sympathies, Blackwood is eager to exaggerate Mary's sufferings: So the two strokes that fell in Wyngfield's account turn into three, "to make her martyrdom the more noble," Blackwood insists, and perhaps also to recall the Holy Trinity. Afterward, the telltale "coif" that slipped of its own volition in Wyngfield's version of events is roughly "pulled off her" by an executioner filled with "derision and contempt," so that instead of denying Mary grace and authority, the spectacle only signifies those qualities together with the magnitude of her recent suffering.

These two competing accounts of the death of Mary Queen of Scots provide a good place for our consideration to end. Beginning with her treason trial and ending with her execution, the last four months of Mary's life bared a profound schism in English social and political life. In sentencing the Queen of Scots to death, Elizabeth confirmed the Protestant course upon which her country was set. For centuries, anti-Catholicism would run rampant in Britain, with persecutions of Catholics on the books until the Catholic Emancipation Act of 1829; in 1688, an English king, James II, would be deposed as much for his Catholic faith as for his infamously autocratic leanings.

The second effect of the trial and execution of Mary Stuart was ironic: With the dangerously Catholic Queen of Scots out of the way, a childless Elizabeth's throne could pass to Mary's own Protestant son, James VI of Scotland.[50] And so it did, upon the Tudor queen's death in 1603. In a way,

---

[50]This ironic line of succession was made possible by the Queen's Safety Act of 1585.

Mary had died in vain. Her family was to inherit the English throne in any case, and the crowns of Scotland and England were thus to be joined after all. In 1707, the Act of Union would certify those countries' economic and political consolidation into the single entity of Great Britain.

Meanwhile, though, the house of Stuart itself was to have a tumultuous and ultimately tragic career upon the English throne: Mary's grandson, Charles I, would lose his own head, James II would be driven from the throne, and in 1714 the direct line of Stuarts — some of whom, like Mary, inclined dangerously to decadent French sensibilities and the Catholic faith — would be replaced by the soberly Protestant and German house of Hanover. We might thus say that Mary's many trials — culminating in her legal one — provided a paradigmatic instance of Stuart unpopularity in England.

Third, Mary's treason trial and subsequent beheading foreshadows the weakening and at last the dismantling of absolute sovereignty in England and Scotland. As they replaced loyalty to a monarch with loyalty to religious creed and conscience, the wars of religion on the European continent had already gravely undermined sovereign power in Europe. Mary's own complicity with Roman Catholic plots against Elizabeth had underscored that weakness, much as her own death had, in a different way, suggested that the days of powerful monarchy might be numbered. In any case, we have seen that Mary's own fate at the hands first of her own subjects in Scotland and then of ambitious Englishmen illustrated the vulnerability of monarchs. Elizabeth, too, ultimately had to yield to the wishes of her Parliament, contrary as they were to at least some of her own impulses and intuitions, and she was well aware that in striking Mary down she was destroying an anointed queen.

Just so, while religious and political turmoil of the sort that had caught both Mary and Elizabeth in its maelstrom was to galvanize absolutism in France, in England the coming Civil Wars of the seventeenth century would result in England's rejection (and later its modification) of the very institution of monarchy. Mary's trial and death seems to have anticipated as much. After her burial at Peterborough Cathedral in August of 1587, an epitaph was erected near her tomb, then swiftly removed for its dangerous political insinuations. For it predicted that "the same wicked sentence" that "doomed [Mary] to a natural Death" guaranteed that "all surviving kings, being made as common people, are subjected to a civil Death."[51]

---

[51] The epitaph is reproduced in full in William Camden, *Annals, or the History of the Most Renowned and Victorious Princesse Elizabeth, Late Queene of England*, trans. R. N. (London, 1635), 385. This is the third edition of Camden's book, first published in Latin, in 1615, as *Annales rerum Anglicarum et hibernicarum regnane Elizabetha*.

But the fourth and final legacy of Mary's trial pertains to queens, not "kings." We saw that, had either Mary or Elizabeth been male, a very different drama would have unfolded between the two of them, quite possibly a comedy ending in marriage rather than a tragedy ending in betrayal and death. We also saw how many of Mary's problems could be traced to the fact that she was a particular kind of woman, one extraordinarily vulnerable to ambitious, clever, and unscrupulous men—both Scottish and English—at a precarious historical moment. Elizabeth's need to guard her reputation as a woman likewise colored her relationship to another female ruler whose death only appeared to guarantee Elizabeth's own life. As they themselves seem to have realized, Elizabeth and Mary represented not only two myths of femininity, but also the sad fact that a complex range of subtle and original possibilities for female identity had to be sacrificed to make room for those myths.

Most, if not all, historians would agree that Mary bore the brunt of this sacrifice, paying for her generation's narrow paradigms of female power with her life. But Elizabeth also paid, and never more fully than in the Mary Stuart affair. Thanks to that affair, her own reputation as a just and honorable queen would be forever mixed. It is only fitting, then, that in 1612 Mary Stuart's body was removed from its first resting place in Peterborough, and at the behest of her son, James, reinterred in London's Westminster Abbey, where Elizabeth herself already lay buried. Today, Mary's tomb stands only a few yards from Elizabeth's own. The two queens who never met in life are joined forever in death.

A NOTE ABOUT THE TEXT

Written English in the time of Elizabeth I and Mary Queen of Scots differs, sometimes dramatically, from written English of the present day. In the interest of clarity and accessibility to the modern reader, the spelling and punctuation of several contemporary documents have been modernized into the style of modern British English. The texts of George Buchanan's *Ane Detection of the Doings of Mary Queen of Scots,* John Leslie's *Defence of the Honour of . . . Marie,* and Adam Blackwood's *History of Mary Queen of Scots* have all been altered accordingly, albeit at no expense to the sense and syntax of the original.

Figure 1. The Ditchley Portrait by Marcus Gheeraerts the Younger (1592), so-called because Elizabeth's foot rests upon Ditchley, Oxfordshire, scene of an elaborate entertainment in her honor in 1592.

Figure 2. Elizabeth I in her coronation robes by an anonymous artist (ca. 1559).

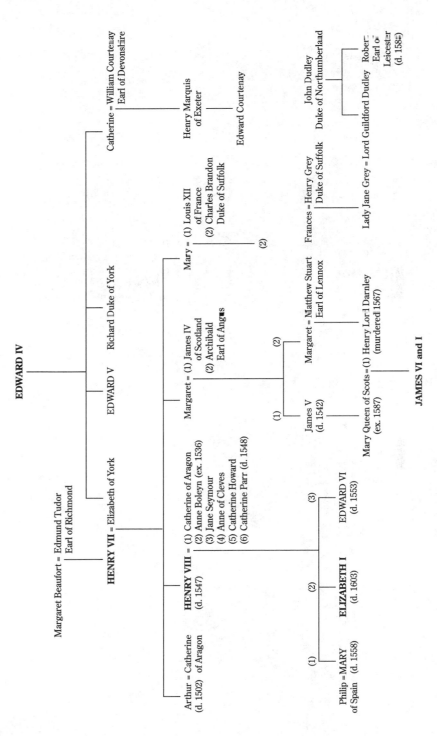

Figure 3. Genealogies of the Tudor and Stuart royal families.

Figure 4. *(left)*   Mary Queen of Scots in "white mourning" by François Clouet (ca. 1559). Mary wears the white clothes and veil associated with mourning in 16th-century France. The occasion of sorrow may have been the death of her father-in-law, Henri II.

Figure 5. *(below left)* Caricature of Mary Queen of Scots, by an anonymous artist, at the time of her elopement to Bothwell. The mermaid was a familiar symbol for a seductress. The rabbit represents Bothwell.

Figure 6. The trial of Mary Queen of Scots, a contemporary engraving. The empty canopied chair at the top represents the absent Queen Elizabeth. At the top right, Mary is being brought in to the trial, but as this scene shows, she is almost excluded from the proceedings.

Figure 7. The Blairs Memorial Portrait of Mary Queen of Scots by an anonymous artist, commissioned after Mary's death by her woman-in-waiting, Elizabeth Curle, who attended her at her execution. Two crucifixes, a missal, and a rosary all mark Mary as a devout Catholic.

PART TWO

The Documents

1

JOHN KNOX

The First Blast of the Trumpet against the Monstrous Regiment of Women

1558

From its title to its final sentence, John Knox's The First Blast of the Trumpet against the Monstrous Regiment of Women *is likely to strike the modern reader as pure venom; it is certainly a radical—even contorted—expression of the misogyny common in Knox's day. Every word of* The First Blast *is devoted to proving that woman is by nature too "weak, frail, impatient, feeble and foolish" to command a scepter. Knox summons natural law, ancient history, and holy scripture to his side, maintaining that since woman was "created to be subject to man," her political rule amounts to an act of treason against a human hierarchy presumably ordained by God.*

Although Knox (1505–72) wrote in the idiom of absolutes, he nonetheless also responded to a specific historical situation. In the 1550s, three Euro-

John Knox. *The First Blast of the Trumpet against the Monstrous Regiment of Women* (Geneva, 1558).

53

pean women wielded considerable political power: Albeit unofficially, the Italian wife of the Valois king, Catherine de Medici, enjoyed enormous influence in France; Mary Tudor occupied the English throne; and Mary Stuart's mother, Marie de Guise, was her daughter's efficient regent in Knox's native Scotland. Besides challenging centuries of exclusively male political authority, all of these women were Roman Catholic: Mary Tudor, the chief target of The First Blast, *openly persecuted her Protestant subjects. By contrast, Knox was one of the most zealous Protestants of his day, a true son of the Reformation that had begun in the early sixteenth century with Martin Luther's rebellion against the pope. Though trained as a Catholic priest, Knox too had revolted against Rome; traveling back and forth between Scotland and the strongly Protestant city of Geneva, he devoted his life to spreading the reformed religion, as well as to the establishment of the Presbyterian Church. Thus while Knox's* First Blast *openly assaulted the institution of female rule, his diatribe was really directed as much against Catholic power as against female authority itself.*

Knox was heavily involved with Scottish politics throughout the personal rule of Mary Stuart, which began two years after The First Blast *was sounded. In the last decades of his life, he was instrumental in the slow erosion of Catholic power in Scotland, and his powerful, impassioned speaking style converted hundreds to the Protestant faith. Knox describes his futile attempt to proselytize the Queen of Scots, whom he loathed, in his later* History of the Reformation in Scotland *(1586–87; 1644).*

The First Blast *was first published in 1558, along with six related treatises; a* Second Blast *was sketched but never completed. It was just as well; the first won the enmity not only of the dying Mary Tudor but also of her half-sister, Elizabeth, who succeeded Mary the very year* The First Blast *was published. Elizabeth banned Knox from England, and, though herself a Protestant, remained hostile to his Presbyterian Church for the rest of her life.*

To promote a Woman to beare rule, superioritie, dominion, or empire above any Realme, Nation, or Citie, is repugnant to Nature; contumelie to God, a thing most contrarious to his reveled will and approved ordinance; and finallie, it is the subversion of good Order, of all equitie and justice.

In the probation of this Proposition, I will not be so curious as to gather what soever may amplifie, set furth, or decore the same; but I am purposed, even as I have spoken my conscience in most plaine and few wordes, so to stand content with a simple proofe of everie membre, bringing in for my witnesse Goddes ordinance in Nature, his plaine will revelled in his Worde, and by the mindes of such as be moste auncient amongest godlie Writers.

And first, where that I affirme the empire of a Woman to be a thing repugnant to Nature, I meane not onlie that God, by the order of his creation, hath spoiled woman of authoritie and dominion, but also that man hath seen, proved, and pronounced just causes why that it shuld be. Man, I say, in many other cases blind, doth in this behalfe see verie clearlie. For the causes be so manifest, that they can not be hid. For who can denie but it is repugneth to nature, that the blind shall be appointed to leade and conduct such as do see? That the weake, the sicke, and impotent persons shall norishe and kepe the hole and strong? And finallie, that the foolishe, madde, and phrenetike shal governe the discrete, and give counsel to such as be sober of mind? And such be al women, compared unto man in bearing of authoritie. For their sight in civile regiment is but blindnes; their strength, weaknes; their counsel, foolishnes; and judgment, phrensy, if it be rightlie considered.

I except such as God, by singular priviledge, and for certain causes, known onlie to himselfe, hath exempted from the common ranke of women, and do speake of women as nature and experience do this day declare them. Nature, I say, doth paynt them furthe to be weake, fraile, impacient, feble, and foolishe; and experience hath declared them to be unconstant, variable, cruell, and lacking the spirit of counsel and regiment. And these notable faultes have men in all ages espied in that kindle, for the whiche not onlie they have removed women from rule and authoritie, but also some have thoght that men subject to the counsel or empire of their wyves were unworthie of all public office. For thus writeth Aristotle in the Seconde of his Politikes: What difference shal we put, saith he, whether that Women beare authoritie, or the husbandes that obey the empire of their wyves, be appointed to be Magistrates? For what insueth the one, must nedes folowe the other, to witte, injustice, confusion, and disorder. The same author further reasoneth, that the policie or regiment of the Lacedemonians[1] (who other wayes amongest the Grecians were moste excellent) was not worthie to be reputed nor accompted amongest the nombre of common welthes that were well governed, because the Magistrates and Rulers of the same were too muche geven to please and obey their wyves. What wolde this writer (I pray you) have said to that realme or nation, where a woman sitteth crowned in Parliament amongest the middest of men? Oh fearefull and terrible are thy judgementes (O Lord) whiche thus hast abased man for his iniquitie! I am assuredlie persuaded that if any of those men, which, illuminated onlie by the light of nature, did see and pronounce causes sufficient why women ought not to beare rule nor authoritie, shuld this day live and see

---

[1]The Spartans, ancient Greeks famed for their austerity and strict discipline, and for their military prowess.

a woman sitting in judgement, or riding frome Parliament in the middest of men, having the royall crowne upon her head, the sworde and sceptre borne before her, in signe that the administration of justice was in her power: I am assuredlie persuaded, I say, that such a sight shulde so astonishe them, that they shulde judge the hole worlde to be transformed into Amazones,[2] and that suche a metamorphosis and change was made of all the men of that countrie, as poetes do feyn was made of the companyons of Ulisses,[3] or at least, that albeit the outwarde form of men remained, yet shuld they judge that their hartes were changed frome the wisdome, understanding, and courage of men, to the foolishe fondnes and cowardise of women. Yea, they further shuld pronounce, that where women reigne or be in authoritie, that there must nedes vanitie be preferred to vertue, ambition and pride to temperancie and modestie; and finallie, that avarice, the mother of all mischefe, must nedes devour equitie and justice. But lest that we shall seme to be of this opinion alone, let us heare what others have seen and decreed in this mater. In the Rules of the Lawe thus it is written: "Women are removed frome all civile and publike office, so that they nether may be Judges, nether may they occupie the place of the Magistrate; nether yet may they be speakers for others." The same is repeted in the Third and in the Sextenth Bookes of the Digestes,[4] where certein persones are forbidden, *Ne pro aliis postulent,* that is, that they be no speakers nor advocates for others. And among the rest are women forbidden, and this cause is added, that they do not against shamefastnes intermedle them selves with the causes of others; nether yet that women presume to use the offices due to men. The Lawe in the same place doth further declare, that a naturall shamfastnes oght to be in womankind, whiche most certeinlie she loseth whensoever she taketh upon her the office and estate of man. As in Calphurnia[5] was evidentlie declared, who having licence to speake before the Senate, at length became so impudent and importune, that by her babling she troubled the whole Assemblie; and so gave occasion that this lawe was established.

In the First Boke of the Digestes, it is pronounced that the condition of the woman in many cases is worse then of the man. As in jurisdiction (saith the Lawe), in receiving of cure and tuition, in adoption, in publike

---

[2] Legendary warlike women of the ancient world who presumably lived without men.

[3] Latin name for Odysseus, the hero of Homer's ancient Greek epic, *The Odyssey*. His travels in the Mediterranean basin on his way home from the Trojan Wars included a visit to the island of Circe, where a witch transformed his men into swine.

[4] Ancient books of Roman law.

[5] Calpurnia, outspoken and devoted wife of Julius Caesar, who addressed the Roman senate.

accusation, in delation, in all popular action, and in motherlie power, which she hath not upon her owne sonnes. The Lawe further will not permit that the woman geve any thing to her husband, because it is against the nature of her kinde, being the inferiour membre, to presume to geve any thing to her head. The Lawe doth more over pronounce womankinde to be most avaricious (which is a vice intolerable in those that shulde rule or minister justice). And Aristotle, as before is touched, doth plainly affirme, that whersoever women beare dominion, there must nedes the people be disordred, livinge and abounding in all intemperancie, geven to pride, excesse, and vanitie; and finallie in the end, that they must nedes come to confusion and ruine.

Wold to God the examples were not so manifest to the further declaration of the imperfections of women, of their naturall weaknes and inordinat appetites! I might adduce histories, proving some women to have died for sodein joy; some for unpacience to have murthered them selves, some to have burned with such inordinat lust, that for the quenching of the same, they have betrayed to strangiers their countrie and citie; and some to have bene so desirous of dominion, that for the obteining of the same, they have murthered the children of their owne sonnes, yea, and some have killed with crueltie their owne husbandes and children. But to me it is sufficient (because this parte of nature is not my moste sure foundation) to have proved, that men illuminated onlie by the light of nature, have seen and have determined, that it is a thing moste repugnant to nature, that women rule and governe over men. For those that will not permit a woman to have power over her owne sonnes, will not permit her (I am assured) to have rule over a realme; and those that will not suffer her to speake in defense of those that be accused, nether that will admit her accusation intended against man, will not approve her that she shal sit in judgement crowned with the royal crowne, usurping authoritie in the middest of men.

But now to the second part of Nature, in the whiche I include the reveled will and perfect ordinance of God; and against this parte of nature, I say, that it doth manifestlie repugne that any Woman shal reigne or beare dominion over man. For God, first by the order of his creation, and after by the curse and malediction pronounced against the woman, by the reason of her rebellion, hath pronounced the contrarie. First, I say, that woman in her greatest perfection was made to serve and obey man, not to rule and command him. As Saint Paule doth reason in these wordes: "Man is not of the woman, but the woman of the man. And man was not created for the cause of the woman, but the woman for the cause of man; and therfore oght the woman to have a power upon her head"[6] (that is, a

[6]A paraphrase of I Corinthians 11:3–4.

coverture in signe of subjection). Of whiche words it is plaine that the Apostle meaneth, that woman in her greatest perfection, shuld have knowen that man was Lord above her; and therfore that she shulde never have pretended any kind of superioritie above him, no more then do the Angels above God the Creator, or above Christ Jesus their head. So I say, that in her greatest perfection, woman was created to be subject to man. But after her fall and rebellion committed against God, there was put upon her a newe necessitie, and she was made subject to man by the irrevocable sentence of God, pronounced in these wordes: "I will greatlie multiplie thy sorowe and thy conception: With sorowe shalt thou beare thy children, and thy will shall be subject to thy man: and he shal beare dominion over thee." Herebie may such as altogether be not blinded plainlie see, that God by his sentence hath dejected all women frome empire and dominion above man. For two punishmentes are laid upon her, to witte, a dolor, anguishe, and payn, as oft as ever she shal be mother; and a subjection of her self, her appetites, and will, to her husband, and to his will. Frome the former parte of this malediction can nether arte, nobilitie, policie, nor lawe made by man, deliver womankinde; but whosoever atteineth to that honour to be mother, proveth in experience the effect and strength of Goddes word. But (alas!) ignorance of God, ambitioun, and tyrannie, have studied to abolishe and destroy the second parte of Goddes punishment. For women are lifted up to be heades over realmes, and to rule above men at their pleasure and appetites. But horrible is the vengeance which is prepared for the one and for the other, for the promoters, and for the persones promoted, except they spedelie repent. For they shall be dejected from the glorie of the sonnes of God to the sclaverie of the Devill, and to the tormente that is prepared for all suche as do exalte them selves against God. Against God can nothing be more manifest then that a woman shall be exalted to reigne above man: for the contrarie sentence hath He pronounced in these wordes: "Thy will shall be subject to thy husband, and he shall beare dominion over thee."[7] As God shuld say, 'Forasmuch as thou hast abused thy former condition, and because thy free will hath broght thy selfe and mankind into the bondage of Satan, I therefore will bring thee in bondage to man. For where before thy obedience shuld have bene voluntarie, nowe it shall be by constreint and by necessitie; and that because thou hast deceived thy man, thou shalt therefore be no longer maistresse over thine own appetites, over thine owne will or desires. For in thee there is nether reason nor discretion whiche be able to moderate

[7]Genesis 3:16.

thy affections, and therfore they shall be subject to the desire of thy man. He shall be Lord and Governour, not onlie over thy bodie, but even over thy appetites and will.' This sentence, I say, did God pronounce against Heva[8] and her daughters, as the rest of the Scriptures doth evidentlie witnesse. So that no woman can ever presume to reigne above man, but the same she must nedes do in despite of God, and in contempt of his punishment and malediction.

I am not ignorant, that the most part of men do understand this malediction of the subjection of the wife to her husband, and of the dominion which he beareth above her; but the Holie Ghost geveth to us an other interpretation of this place, taking from all women all kinde of superioritie, authoritie, and power over man, speaking as foloweth by the mouth of Saint Paule: "I suffer not a woman to teache, nether yet to usurpe authoritie above man."[9] Here he nameth women in generall, excepting none; affirming that she may usurpe authoritie above no man. And that he speaketh more plainlie in an other place in these wordes: "Let women kepe silence in the Congregation, for it is not permitted to them to speake, but to be subject, as the lawe sayeth."[10] These two testimonies of the Holy Ghost be sufficient to prove what soever we have affirmed before, and to represse the inordinate pride of women, as also to correct the foolishnes of those that have studied to exalt women in authoritie above men, against God and against his sentence pronounced. But that the same two places of the Apostle may the better be understand, it is to be noted, that in the latter, which is written in the First Epistle to the Corinthes, the 14 chapitre, before the Apostle had permitted that all persones shuld prophecie one after an other, addinge this reason, "that all may learne and all may receive consolation;" and lest that any might have judged, that amongest a rude multitude, and the pluralitie of speakers, manie thinges litle to purpose might have bene affirmed, or elles that some confusion might have risen, he addeth, "The spirites of the prophetes are subject to the prophetes;" as he shuld say, God shall alwayes raise up some to whome the veritie shal be reveled, and unto such ye shal geve place, albeit they sit in the lowest seates. And thus the Apostle wold have prophesying an exercise to be free to the hole Churche, that everie one shuld communicate with the Congregation what God had reveled to them, providinge that it were orderlie done. But frome this generall priviledge he secludeth all women, saying, "Let women kepe silence in the Congregation." And why, I pray you? Was it because that the Apostle thoght no woman to have any knowledge? No;

[8]Eve.
[9]I Timothy 2:8.
[10]I Corinthians 14:34.

he geveth an other reason, saying, "Let her be subject, as the lawe saith." In which wordes is first to be noted, that the Apostle calleth this former sentence pronounced against woman a lawe, that is, the immutable decree of God, who by his owne voice hath subjected her to one membre of the Congregation, that is to her husband. Wherupon the Holie Ghost concludeth, that she may never rule nor bear empire above man: for she that is made subject to one, may never be preferred to many. And that the Holie Ghoste doth manifestlie expresse, saying: "I suffer not that woman usurpe authoritie above man"; he sayth not, I will not that woman usurpe authoritie above her husband, but he nameth man in generall, taking from her all power and authoritie to speake, to reason, to interprete, or to teache; but principallie to rule or to judge in the assemblie of men. So that woman by the lawe of God, and by the interpretation of the Holy Ghost, is utterly forbidden to occupie the place of God in the offices afore said, which he hath assigned to man, whome he hath appointed and ordeined his lieutenant in earth, secluding frome that honor and dignitie all women, as this short argument shall evidentlie declare. . . .

[*Knox's "argument" proves less "short" than he makes it out to be, and* The First Blast *here lapses into a long harangue against French and Spanish tyranny, coupled with a reiteration of scriptural injunctions against female rule and an incidental sneer at female fondness for "gorgeous apparel." Knox then turns back to the main subject at hand, and addresses the fact that traditionally women have held power in several societies, ancient and modern.*]

The Consent, say they, of realmes and lawes pronounced and admitted in this behalfe, long consuetude[11] and custome, together with the felicitie of some Women in their empires, have established their Authoritie. To whome I answer, that nether may the tyrannie of princes, nether the foolishnes of people, nether wicked lawes made against God, nether yet the felicitie that in this earthe may herof insue, make that thing laufull which he by his Word hath manifestlie condemned. For if the approbation of princes and people, and lawes made by men, or the consent of realmes, may establishe any thing against God and his Word, then shuld idolatrie be preferred to the true religion; for mo[12] realmes and nations, mo lawes and decrees published by Emperours with common consent of their counsels, have established the one then have approved the other: And yet I thinke that no man of sounde judgement will therfore justifie and defend idolatrie; no more oght any man to mainteine this odious

---

[11]Custom, tradition of social usage.
[12]More.

empire of Women, although that it were approved of all men by their lawes. For the same God, that in plain wordes forbiddeth idolatrie, doth also forbidde the authoritie of women over man; as he wordes of Saint Paule before rehearsed do plainly teach us. And therfore, whether women be deposed from that unjust Authoritie (have they never usurped it so long,) or if all such honour be denied unto them, I feare not to affirme that they are nether defrauded of right nor inheritance. For to Woman can that honour never be due nor laufull (muche lesse inheritance) whiche God hath so manifestlie denied unto them.

I am not ignorant that the subtill wittes of carnall men (which can never be broght under the obedience of Goddes simple preceptes) to maintein this monstruous empire have yet two vaine shiftes. First, they alledge, that albeit Women may not absolutclic rcigne by themselves, because they may nether sit in judgement, nether pronounce sentence, nether execute any publike office, yet may they do all such thinges by their lieutenantes, deputies, and judges substitute. Secondarilie, say they, a Woman borne to rule over any realme may chose her a husband, and to him she may transfer and geve her authoritie and right. To both I answer in fewe wordes. First, That frome a corrupt and venomed fountein can spring no holsome water. Secondarilie, That no person hath power to geve the thing which doth not justlie appertein to them selves: But the authoritie of a woman is a corrupted fountein, and therfore from her can never spring any lauful officer. She is not borne to rule over men, and therfore she can apointe none by her gift, nor by her power (which she hath not), to the place of a laufull Magistrat; and therfore, who soever receiveth of a woman office or authoritie, are adulterous and bastard officers before God. This may appeare straunge at the first affirmation, but if we will be as indifferent and equall in the cause of God as that we can be in the cause of man, the reason shall sodeinlie appeare. The case supposed, that a tyranne by conspiracie usurped the royall seat and dignitie of a King, and in the same did so establish him selfe, that he apointed officers, and did what him list for a time; and in this meane time the native King made streit inhibition to all his subjects, that none shuld adhere to this traitor, nether yet receive any dignitie of him; yet, neverthelesse, they wold honour the same traitor as King, and become his officers in all affaires of the realme. If after the native Prince did recover his just honour and possession, shuld he repute or esteme any man of the traitor's apointment for a laufull Magistrate, or for his frende and true subject? Or shuld he not rather with one sentence condemne the head with the membres? And if so he shuld do, who were able to accuse him of rigour, much lesse to condemne his sentence of injustice? And dare we denie the same power to God in the like case? For that Woman reigneth above man, she hath obtained it by treason and conspiracie committed against God.

How can it be then, that she, being criminall and giltie of treason against God committed, can apoint any officer pleasing in his sight? It is a thing impossible. Wherfore, let men that receive of women authoritie, honor, or office, be most assuredly persuaded, that in so mainteining that usurped power, they declare themselves ennemies to God. If any thinke, that because the Realme and Estates therof have geven their consentes to a woman, and have established her and her authoritie, that therfore it is laufull and acceptable before God, let the same men remembre what I have said before, to wit, that God can not approve the doing nor consent of any multitude, concluding any thing against his worde and ordinance; and therfore they must have a more assured defence against the wrath of God then the approbation and consent of a blinded multitude, or elles they shall not be able to stand in the presence of the consuming fire: That is, they must acknowledge that the Regiment of a Woman is a thing most odious in the presence of God; they must refuse to be her officers, because she is a traitoresse and rebell against God; and finallie, they must studie to represse her inordinate pride and tyrannie to the uttermost of their power.

The same is the dutie of the Nobilitie and Estates, by whose blindnes a Woman is promoted. First, in so farre as they have moste haynouslie offended against God, placing in authoritie suche as God by his Worde hath removed frome the same, unfeinedly they oght to call for mercie; and, being admonished of their error and damnable fact, in signe and token of true repentance, with common consent, they oght to retreate that which unadvisedlie and by ignorance they have pronounced; and oght, without further delay, to remove from authority all such persones as by usurpation, violence, or tyrannie, do possesse the same. For so did Israel and Juda after they had revolted from David, and Juda alone in the dayes of Athalia.[13] For after that she, by murthering her sonnes children, had obteined the empire over the land, and had most unhappelie reigned in Juda six years, Jehoiada the High priest called together the capitaines and chief rulers of the people, and shewing to them the Kinges sonne Joas, did binde them by an othe to depose that wicked woman, and to promote the King to his royall seat; which they faithfullie did, killing at his commandement not onlie that cruell and mischevous woman, but also the people did destroie the temple of Baal, break his altars and images, and kill Mathan, Baales High priest, before his altars.

The same is the dutie aswell of the Estates as of the People that hath bene blinded. First, They oght to remove frome honour and authoritie that monstre in nature: So call I a woman cled in the habit of man, yea, a

---

[13]Daughter of Ahab and Jezebel, married to the king of ancient Judah. After his death and that of her son, Athalia usurped the throne and reigned for seven years, during which time she had most of the members of the royal household massacred. This bloodthirsty Old Testament queen was herself killed in a revolution. Her story is told in II Kings.

woman against nature reigning above man. Secondarilie, If any presume to defende that impietie, they oght not to feare first to pronounce, and then after to execute against them the sentence of deathe. If any man be affraid to violat the oth of obedience which they have made to suche monstres, let them be most assuredly persuaded, that as the beginning of their othes, proceding from ignorance, was sinne, so is the obstinate purpose to kepe the same nothing but plaine rebellion against God. But of this mater in THE SECOND BLAST, God willing, we shall speake more at large.

And nowe, to put an end to THE FIRST BLAST: Seing that by the ordre of Nature; by the malediction and curse pronounced against Woman, by the mouth of S. Paule, the interpreter of Goddes sentence; by the example of that Common welth in whiche God by his Word planted ordre and policie; and finallie, by the judgement of the most godlie writers, God hath dejected woman frome rule, dominion, empire, and authoritie above man: Moreover, seing that nether the example of Debora, nether the lawe made for the doughters of Zalphead, nether yet the foolishe consent of an ignorant multitude, be able to justifie that whiche God so plainlie hath condemned; let all men take hede what quarell and cause frome hencefurthe they do defend. If God raise up any noble harte to vendicat the libertie of his Countrie, and to suppresse the monstruous empire of Women, but all suche as shal presume to defend them in the same moste certeinlie knowe, that in so doing they lift their hand against God and that one day they shall finde his power to fight against their foolishnes.

2

GEORGE BUCHANAN

Ane Detection of the Doings of
Mary Queen of Scots

1571

The Scottish Protestant educator George Buchanan's Detection of the Doings of Mary Queen of Scots *is rooted in the legal actions taken against Mary Stuart shortly after the end of her personal rule in Scotland. In this vehement treatise, Buchanan (1506–82) provides an eyewitness account*

George Buchanan. *A Detection of the Actions of Mary Queen of Scots* (London, 1725). Originally published in 1571 as *Ane Detection of the Doings of Mary Queen of Scots.*

of Mary's allegedly scandalous behavior during her brief, stormy second marriage to the English Catholic Henry, Lord Darnley. Darnley had died under mysterious circumstances in February 1567, and shortly thereafter Mary had eloped with the man believed responsible for his death, James Hepburn, Earl of Bothwell. She was imprisoned by her own subjects and eventually deposed. When she fled to England, Elizabeth Tudor promptly put her under lock and key, and an English commission met at York in 1568 to hear a Scottish contingent's charges that the Queen of Scots had both committed adultery with Bothwell and conspired with him to put an end to Darnley.

The verdict was ambiguous; Mary was found neither guilty nor innocent, and for mostly other reasons went on to nineteen years of captivity on English soil. The Scottish delegation went back home. But out of the trial proceedings, an important document, known as the Book of Articles, emerged—an eyewitness account of Mary's alleged misdeeds, indiscretions, and abuses of power during her marriage to Darnley. The Book was meant to be read in conjunction with a collection of sonnets and love letters that Mary had presumably written to Bothwell during her marriage to Lord Darnley. (Known as the Casket Letters because they were allegedly housed in a gilt box, these documents disappeared suspiciously soon and many doubt that they ever existed.)

The author of the Book of Articles, Buchanan, had known Mary during her girlhood in France, where he had tutored her and even written a warm epithalamium celebrating her first marriage to the French dauphin, François II. He had also frequented Mary's court in Edinburgh, and there had become a favorite of her ambitious Protestant half-brother, the Earl of Moray. It was with Moray's support that Buchanan produced his Book of Articles; he later polished the work and in 1571 he published it, in Latin, along with copies and translations of the Casket Letters, under the title Detectio: sive de Maria. *The Detectio was later translated into English as* Ane Detection of the Doings of Mary Queen of Scots *and reprinted several times. Its lurid central image of a queen overruled by her own lust for power and sex— "a woman," Buchanan says, "raging weathout measure and modesty"—is the foundation of one enduring popular image of Mary Queen of Scots as a lascivious and bloodthirsty adulteress.*

Buchanan's Detection, *whose text has here been modernized, berates Mary for abusing the laws of proper femininity—indeed, for "the undoing of all laws" in the pursuit of personal gratification. It thus voices an anxiety about female sovereignty (and woman's inevitable abuse of power) akin to John Knox's. The* Detection *justifies Mary's deposition and, implicitly, her captivity by Elizabeth Tudor, arguing that "we deprived [Mary] not of liberty, but of unbridled licentiousness of evil doing." Note Buchanan's rhetorical and linguistic self-consciousness—a quality he later bequeathed to his most famous pupil, Mary's Protestant son, James VI of Scotland and I of England.*

. . . Albeit these things [i.e., the murder of Mary's husband, Darnley, her adultery, and later elopement with his supposed killer, Bothwell] were thus done as I have declared, yet there are some that stick not to say that the Queen was not only hardly, but also cruelly dealt with, that after so detestable a fact, she was removed from her regency, and when they [i.e., Mary's supporters] could not deny the fact they complained of the punishment. I do not think there will be any man so shameless to think that so horrible a fact ought to have no punishment at all. But if they complain of the grievousness of the penalty, I fear lest, to all good men, we may seem not to have done so gently and temperately, as loosely and negligently, that have laid so light a penalty upon an offence so heinous, and such as was never heard of before.

For what can be done cruelly against the author of so outrageous a deed, wherein all laws of God and man are violated, despised, and in a manner wholly extinguished? Every several offence hath its punishment both by God and man appointed: And as there be certain degrees of evil deeds, so are there also increases in the quantities of punishments. If one has killed a man, it is a deed of itself very heinous. What if he has killed his familiar friend? What if his father? What if in one foul fact he hath joined all these offences together? Surely of such a one, neither can his life suffice for imposing, nor his body for bearing, nor the Judges' policy for inventing pain enough for him. Which of these faults is not comprised in this offence? I omit the mean common matters—the murdering of a young gentleman, an innocent, her countryman, her kinsman, her familiar, and her cousin german.[1] Let us also excuse the fact, if it be possible. She unadvisedly, a young woman, angry, offended, and one of great innocency of life till this time, hath slain a lewd young man, and adulterer, and unkind husband, and a cruel King.

If not any one, but all these respects together were in this matter, they ought not to avail to shift off all punishment, but to raise some pity of the case. But what say you that none of these things can so much as be falsely pretended? The fact itself, of itself, is odious: In a woman, it is monstrous: In a wife not only excessively loved, but also most zealously honoured, it is incredible.

And being committed against him whose age craved pardon, whose hearty affection required love, whose nighness of kindred asked reverence, whose innocency might have deserved favour, upon that young man I say, in whom there is not so much alleged as any just cause of offence,

---

[1] Literally a first cousin, but here it refers only to the fact that Mary and Darnley were distantly related.

thus to execute and spend—yea, to exceed all torments due to all offences—in what degree of cruelty shall we account it?

But let these things avail in other persons to raise hatred, to bring punishment, and to make examples to posterity. But in this case let us bear much with her youth, much with her nobility, much with the name of a princess. As for mine own part, I am not one that thinks it always good to use extreme strictness of law, no, not in private, mean and common persons. But in a most heinous misdeed, to dissolve all force of law, and where is no measure of ill-doing, there to descend beneath all measure in punishing, were the way to the undoing of all laws, and the overthrow of all human society. But in this one horrible act is such a hodgepodge of all abominable doings, such an eagerness of all outrageous cruelty, such a forgetfulness of all natural affection, as nothing more can be feigned or imagined. I omit all former matters.

I will not curiously inquire upon princes' doings; I will not weigh them by the common beam, I will not restrain them to common degrees of duties. If there be anything that without great offence may be passed over, I will gladly leave it unspoken of; if there be anything that may receive excuse, either by respect of age or of womankind, yea or of unadvisedness, I will not urge it.

And to pass over all the rest, two heinous offences there be that, neither according to their greatness be fully expressed, nor according to their outrage, be sufficiently punished. I mean the violating of matrimony and of royal majesty. For matrimony (as the Apostle saith) doth truly contain a great mystery. For, as being observed, it compriseth within it all inferior kinds of duties, so being broken, it overthroweth them all. Whoso hath misused his father seemeth to cast out of his heart all natural reverence, but for the husband's sake *one shall love both father and mother.* Of all other duties, the degrees, or like observances, either are not at all in brute creatures, or not so plain to be discerned. But of matrimonial love, there is almost no living creature that hath not some feeling. This mystery, therefore, whoso not only violateth, but also despiseth, he doth not only overthrow all the foundations of human fellowship; but, as much as in him lieth, dissolveth and confoundeth all order of nature.

Whosoever (I do not say) hurteth the King, that is the true Image of God in earth, but slayeth him with strange and unwonted sort of cruelty, so as the intemperate and incredible outrageousness is not contented with simple torment: Seemeth he not, as much as in him lieth, to have a desire to pull God out of Heaven? What refuge have they then left themselves to mercy, that in satisfying their lust of unjust hatred, have exceeded not only all measure of cruelty, but also all likelihood, that it can be credible?

But, they will say, we ought to bear with, and spare her nobility, dignity and age. Be it so, if she have spared him in whom all these respects were greater, or at least equal. Let the majesty of royal name avail her. How much it ought to avail to her preserving, herself hath shewed the example. May we commit our safety to her, who a sister, hath butcherly slaughtered her brother, a wife her husband, a Queen her King? May we commit our safety to her, whom never shame restrained from unchastity, womankind from cruelty, nor religion from impiety? Shall we bear with her age, sex and unadvisedness, that without all just causes of hatred, despised all these things in her kinsman, her King, her husband?

She that hath sought such execution of her wrongful wrath, what shall we think she will do being provoked by reproaches of men not knit to her by kindred, subject to her pleasure, not matched with her in equal fellowship of life, but yielded to her governance, and enthralled to her tormenting cruelty? When rage for interrupting her pleasure, and outrage of nature, strengthened with armour of licentious power, shall ragingly triumph upon the goods and blood of poor subjects? What is then the fault whereof we are accused? What cruelties have we shewed? That a woman raging without measure and modesty, and abusing to all her subjects' destruction the force of her power, that she had received for their safety, we have kept under governance of her kinsmen and well-willing friends; and whom by right, we might for her heinous deeds have executed: Her we have touched with no other punishment, but only restrained her from doing more mischief. For we deprived her not of liberty, but of unbridled licentiousness of evil doing. Wherein we more fear among all good men the blame of too much lenity than among evil men the slander of cruelty.

3

JOHN LESLIE, BISHOP OF ROSS

A Defence of the Honour of . . . Marie
1569

The Scottish Catholic John Leslie, Bishop of Ross (1527–86), was Mary Stuart's most loyal, ardent, and prolific advocate throughout her English captivity. Educated, like the Queen of Scots, in France, Ross had returned to Scotland in 1554, at which time he became heavily involved in Roman

John Leslie, Bishop of Ross. *A Defence of the Honour of . . . Marie* (London, 1569).

Catholic resistance to the increasing power of Scottish Presbyterians, led by John Knox. After holding a privileged position at Scotland's University of Aberdeen, he became Bishop of Ross, but his dedication to Mary during her Scottish and English captivities resulted in the loss of the bishopric. Ross went on to act as Mary's defense counsel during the hearings at York, and remained an important link between the queen and Scotland throughout her confinement in England. He was twice arrested and imprisoned for his suspected involvement in plots against Elizabeth Tudor; Elizabeth's apparent admiration for Ross and a paucity of direct evidence against him led to his release both times, and he continued to negotiate with Elizabeth for Mary's release, traveling also to the continent in the 1580s to rally support for the Queen of Scots.

Although Ross disapproved of Mary Stuart's rash third marriage to Bothwell, his devotion to her never wavered, and he wrote several treatises asserting her virtue and right of rule between the late 1560s and the early 1580s. Of these, the best known is his 1569 Defence of the Honour of the Right High, Mighty and Noble Princess Marie Queen of Scotland—*a three-part treatise that, though suppressed in England, was eventually printed in France and smuggled back across the English Channel. Leslie's* Defence, *here modernized, was reprinted in 1571 under a different (and slightly less unwieldy) title. Its initial assertion and illumination of the personal virtues of Mary Stuart evolve into an eloquent and substantial defense of female sovereignty generally. Leslie's advocacy of women's rule places him in direct opposition to John Knox, and may explain why he actually found a measure of favor with Elizabeth Tudor. Ironically, Ross also had much in common with Mary's enemy George Buchanan: Both were men of singular erudition, authors of influential histories of their native Scotland, and emotionally invested in the fate of Mary Queen of Scots.*

The first section of Leslie's Defence *proper moves from an eloquent and specific panegyric to Mary as the very definition of female virtue; Part II argues for her right to the English throne (after Elizabeth's death); Part III, excerpted here along with Leslie's preface, ends with a long and eloquent assertion that the "women's regiment" is "conformable both to the law of God, and the law of nature." From beginning to end, Leslie is aware that what he says about Mary applies to Elizabeth as well. Indeed, as he calls for Mary to be acknowledged next in line to Elizabeth's throne, even his preface spotlights the places where the two women's identities virtually overlap. Mary is Elizabeth's "most nigh neighbor by place. And her nigh cousin and sister by blood." She is even "as it were her daughter."*

Leslie had plenty of readers and supporters, and his Defence *counterpoints the misogyny of Knox and Buchanan.*

The Author to the Gentle Reader

It is not unknown to the gentle reader, being an Englishman, what great contention hath of late risen in England, what hot schools and disputations have been kept in many places here, touching the right heir apparent of the crown of England, if God call to his mercy our gracious Queen and Sovereign Elizabeth, without issue of her body. Neither hath this stir stood within the list of earnest and fervent talk of each side, but men have gone on farther, and have as well by printed as unprinted books done their endeavour to disgrace, blemish and deface, as much as it them listeth, the just title, claim and interest of the noble and excellent Lady Marie Queen of Scotland, to the aforesaid crown: Yea, they have in uttering their gross ignorance—or rather their spiteful malice against her grace—run so on headlong that they have expressly denied and refused all womanly government. Among other[s], one of [these] rash, hot, hasty and heady companions hath cast abroad about July last a poisoned pestiferous pamphlet against the said Queen's claim and interest, wherein he announceth also that the civil regiment of women is repugnant both to the law of nature, and to the law of God.[1]

It is moreover well known to all England and Scotland what a business and stir there hath been, what earnest, vehement and violent talk, what false feigned and forged reports and opprobrious slanders have been bruited, as well in the one as in the other realm,[2] against the said virtuous good innocent Lady and Queen, by the crafty malicious drift of her rebellious subjects. Who have not only blown abroad, and filled men's ears with loathsome and heinous accusations against her grace, touching the slaughter of her late dear husband, but have also upon this false slanderous crimination taken arms against her, imprisoned her, and spoiled her of all manner her costly apparel and jewels, and also bereaved her of her princely and royal authority, intruding themselves into the same, under the name and shadow of the young Prince her son.[3]

Touching all these points, ye shall have now, good reader, in this treatise following divided into three books, an answer. And for as much as Solomon writeth, and this good Lady so taketh it, that a good name is to be praised and valued above all precious ornaments, above all gold and

---

[1]The pamphlet Leslie probably had in mind—and refutes throughout his *Defence*—was likely the anonymous *Allegations of the Surmised Title of the Queen of Scots,* recently published in the tradition of Knox's *First Blast.* Leslie indirectly attacks Knox throughout his treatise, and probably also had George Buchanan in mind, Buchanan's *Detection* having been finished and circulated in limited circles at the time Leslie wrote his *Defence.*

[2]I.e., in both England and Scotland.

[3]Leslie refers to the murder of Darnley and to the forced demission of Mary's crown at Lochleven, at which point the monarchy passed to her infant son.

silver,[4] and that the impairing of her honour by these foul and slanderous reports, doth touch and nip her heart nearer than may the loss of any worldly honour, hanging upon her by expectation, or that she hath enjoyed, or doth presently enjoy, or any other grievous injuries that she hath most wrongfully but most patiently suffered.

It is thought good that the defence of her honour should [require] the other two books, whereof the former entreatheth, debatheth and discusseth the right, title and interest of the said Queen Marie, to the succession of this crown of England, declaring her said right and title to be good and lawful, but the common law of this realm, and the acts of parliament therein held. [. . . In the third book of the *Defence*], we avouch woman's regiment to be conformable both to the law of God, and the law of nature. Which treatise may seem perchance to some as superfluous, neither I greatly deny it, and therefore might, and would gladly have spared so much labour and travail, if this little poisoned pamphlet[5] had not many readers, and also many savourers and allowers, or if the matter did not so nigh touch even our own gracious and noble sovereign, or if this lewd assertion were not . . . with the countenance of the law of nature and God's holy word underpropped, or if that God's holy word were not nowadays wretchedly applied (God reform it) and licentiously wreathed and wrested to the maintenance of every private man's fancy and folly, and as fondly and foolishly credited and embraced also of other fantastical persons, or if this man were the first, or like to be the last maintainer and setter forth of such a strange and dangerous Paradox. Or if there have not already been published and divulged by print English books, for the maintenance of the said strange doctrine. . . .

For this and other causes, we have set in the last book a confutation of this gross and dangerous error, whereas also he inveigheth most slanderously against her highness for the aforesaid slaughter with bare naked but spiteful reproaches and outcries, without any manner of kind or countenance of good prose, we will refer the Reader to the aforesaid defence of her honour. By the answer ye shall see her integrity and innocency, and with all that her accusers have in this matter played such a tragedy against their guiltless lady and gracious sovereign, as lightly the world hath not heard of the like. The which their false, slanderous, outrageous,

---

[4]Wise king of the Old Testament, and author of its book of Proverbs. Proverbs 22:1 says that "a good name is rather to be chosen than great riches, and loving favor rather than silver or gold."

[5]*Allegations,* but also implicitly Knox's *First Blast.*

rebellious doings, it is hoped that our gracious queen[6] will well consider and ponder, and will take some convenient order also, as well for the repressing of them, as for the restitution of the said Queen Marie to her own realm. And the rather because our said Queen is learned, and therefore not ignorant what great commendation and immortal fame many kings have purchased to themselves for such benefit bestowed upon other princes, being in the like distress and extremity. The monuments of antiquity, as well profane as ecclesiastical, are filled with the memory of such noble acts. . . .

For this Lady and Queen [Mary] is her most nigh neighbour by place: And her nigh cousin and sister by blood. She is a Queen, and therefore this were a fit benefit for her relief from a Queen. Yea she is, as it were her daughter, both by daughterly reverence she beareth her majesty, and by reason she is of God called to the daughter's place in the succession of the crown, if her majesty fail of issue. And I doubt nothing, if she employ this motherly benefit upon her, but that [Elizabeth] shall find [Mary] a mindful, thankful, and obedient daughter. For of all women in this world, [Mary] abhorreth ingratitude. She hath hitherto depended only upon the hope to have help and succour of her majesty, going over, partly voluntary, partly at the motion of her majesty, diverse proffers of aid and succour by other mighty and puissant Princes, her friends freely to her offered, reposing herself upon the fair and princely promises that her Majesty hath made to her sundry times as well by letters, as by messengers, for her relief, whensoever opportunity should occasion her to crave it. For this and many other considerations, there is good hope, as is aforesaid, that our gracious Mistress will take in hand her restitution. Whereupon, I trust, shall follow such farther and entire amity between them both, and their realms, that the benefit, fruit, and commodity thereof shall plentifully redound, as well to all the posterity of both the said realms hereafter, as to us presently.

From Book III

[Knox and his followers had based a large part of their argument against female "regiment" on a passage in the Old Testament book of Deuteronomy that seems to prohibit women's rule: "You shall surely set a king over you whom the Lord your god chooses; one from among your brethren you shall set as king over you;

---

[6]For rhetorical effect, Leslie throughout speaks from the perspective of both an English and a Scottish subject.

you may not set a foreigner over you, who is not your brother" (Deuteronomy 17:15). Opponents of female sovereignty interpreted "among your brethren" (in Latin, ex fratribus*) literally, holding it to apply only to men.*]

Our good quiet brother doth so strain and wrest this word *(ex fratribus)* among the brethren that he wresteth away not only the right and interest the Queen of Scots pretendeth to the succession of the crown: But doth wrest withal the crowns from all princes' necks that have been, are, or shall be women. And of all such as have, do, or shall claim their inheritance, by the title and interest of their mothers, which can have no better title, than their progenitors from whom they claim. For among his new notable notes that he noteth out of this seventh chapter of Deuteronomy, for the choosing of a king, we may note (sayeth he) the sex by the masculine gender used in this word *ex fratribus*, for under the other *sex ataxia*[7] most commonly creepeth into the stock and country.

He sayeth also afterward, This politic law that God did give the Jews is grounded upon the law of nature, and is also as everlasting as nature itself is, and is of all natural men to be observed. It is (sayeth he) of nature that the prescribed sex should govern the other: He meaneth women should be governed. Then he knotteth up the conclusion of his new pestiferous policy, [by] which I conclude that God's law, nature and good reason do reject the Queen of Scots and deny her that kingdom which she would so fain possess.

Who would ever have thought that such a quiet sober brain, out of this one word *fratris,* could have found in his heart so unbrotherly, yea so unchristianly and so fondly withal, to extort such an interpretation, as is able (if it were received) to disturb, infringe, and break the quiet and lawful possession and inheritance of a great part of the princes of the world, and especially of his own and our gracious and sovereign, good Lady and Queen? Yea and as fondly and unnaturally to frame of himself a new law of nature also: And most wretchedly to corrupt, deprave, and maim both the law of God and nature. Yet because this man giveth out his matters as it were compendious oracles, and lest some might think, that such a sober man hath some good and substantial ground in this his saying — seeing he is so bold with his own glosses upon the holy scriptures — I will be as bold upon him a little, to sift and examine the weight and verity of them. And first touching the law of nature, which he maketh as a pick axe to undermine the state of so many princes, and of his own sovereign

[7] Discord.

withal: We might here enlarge many things how and in what sort the law of nature may be taken; but we will be therein compendious and short.

The law of nature commonly is proper and appertaining as well to other living things as to man. As Ulpian the noble lawyer[8] writeth, there is another law that is called *jus gentium,* the law of all nations,[9] and it is called also the law of nature, because the discourse of natural reason forceth all nations to obey and keep this law, as to honour God, to obey our parents and magistrates, to keep and maintain our bargains and promises of buying and selling, and in other contracts, to defend ourselves from violence and injury, with a number of such other. I suppose the adversary meaneth not of the first kind, but of the second: Whereof he must needs mean, if he mean to speak anything to the purpose. I say then that his is a false and an unnatural assertion, to make this surmised law everlasting as nature itself is. The law of nature, or *jus gentium,* is and ever was after the time that there were any nations or people, and ever shall be. This counterfeit law of nature neither is, nor ever was, nor as far as reason may reach to, ever shall be.

Yet shall be enough for us to throw and cast underfoot this counterfeit law, to show and prove that women have from time to time borne princely regiment in the most notable parts in the world, and in the best and most famous commonwealths that have ever been. For the knowledge whereof, I refer the Reader to ancient histories, being the noble registers of antiquity, which do plainly testify the same to have been often practiced in Asia, Africa, and Europe. Concerning Asia, I find that Artemisia who built the sepulcher of her husband Mausolus (one of the notable spectacles and wonders of the world), and her sister Ada with others reigned in Caria.[10] . . . The government of the Queen Semiramis and Nicocris in the empire of Babylon.[11] . . . In the stories and monuments touching Africa, we read of Queen Dido at Carthage,[12] Cleopatra in Egypt, and divers other queens there. The first king of Egypt was Osiris, who in his absence committed the whole regiment to his wife Isis. In Ethiopia where reigneth a mighty prince, a Christian man, and one that hath many

---

[8]Domitius Ulpianus, a noted Roman jurist of the third century A.D.

[9]Literally, "the law of the people."

[10]A country in southwest Asia Minor. Its king, Mausolus (377–53 B.C.), was married to his own sister, Artemisia, who after his death ordered a splendid tomb for him; hence our word "mausoleum." Widowed, she reigned over Caria and was known as a patroness of the arts.

[11]Semilegendary queen who ruled Babylon for five years (810–05 B.C.) after her husband's death, serving as her son's regent until he came of age and winning fame for her war exploits and city building.

[12]Dido's finally tragic rule of Carthage is recounted in Virgil's *Aeneid.*

kings subjected to him, not many years since in the nonage of King David, his grandmother the Queen did most politicly, wisely and godly rule these realms. And it appeareth in the old stories that in Christ's time and before, that country had no other princes than women, which were called all Candaces. Such a one reigned there about the time of Christ's passion, whose chief servant was converted to Christ's faith by Saint Philip. . . . In the time of King Solomon, the noble woman that came from the uttermost part of the earth to hear the wisdom of the said Solomon, whom the Old Testament calleth the Queen of Sheba . . . was a queen, and as Josephus writeth, the Queen of Ethiopia and Egypt, countries of such greatness and largeness, as no one Prince throughout all our empire, hath so ample dominion with the same. Perchance her dominion did stretch to Cephala, which draweth well toward the farthest part of Africa. . . .

We knit up therefore our conclusion against you after this sort: That law and usage cannot be counted against the law of nature, or *jus gentium,* which the most part of all countries, and one great or notable part of the whole world doth and hath ever used. But this law or usage is such, *ergo* it is not against the law of nature. The *major* needeth no proof: As for the proof of the *minor,* we need to employ no farther labour, than we have already done. Whereupon the consequence must needs be inferred, that this law or usage doth well agree and stand with the law of nature. The reason thereof is, that it is more natural, the daughter to inherit her father's patrimony, whereunto if there be a dignity[13] annexed, both are so united and knit together, that they can in no wise be unlinked.

Marie, if you had driven your argument of the duty and obedience that the wife oweth to her husband, and had argued, it is the law of nature, that the wife should be ruled and governed by her husband, *ergo* it is against nature, that the wife should be head to her husband in respect that she is his wife: then had you argued conformably to reason, scripture, and nature. But if you will thereof infer, *ergo* she can in no wise be head to her husband, then play you the Sophister,[14] making a fallible and vicious argument, and making a confused mingling of those things, that be of sundry and divers natures. . . . The wife may without any impairing or maiming of her duty to God, or to her wedlock, repress her husband's misdemeanor, if it be [noxious] to the commonwealth: And yet is she not

---

[13]An honorary title, such as "Lady," "Countess," or even "Queen."
[14]One of an ancient Greek class of rhetoricians infamous for their ethical relativism and ability to twist any argument to make any point.

thereby exempted from such duty, as the matrimonial conjunction craveth of the wife toward her husband.

Ye frame another argument of inconveniences, as though under the woman's regiment, Ataxia (that is to say disorder) most commonly creepeth in. I will not deny, but sometimes it is so, but that most commonly it is so, that I deny. Let both the regiments be compared and matched together, and weighed by an indifferent balance, and I am deceived, but the inconveniences of the man's regiment for the rate will overpass the other. And it is full meet unseemly and dangerous matter to rule princes' right and titles by such blind guesses.

Well you will yet say, ye have scripture on your side. You say the Jews were commanded to take no king but *ex fratribus,* a brother. *Ergo* we can have no sister to [be] our Queen. To this objection also my two former answers may sufficiently serve. First you must prove, that all Christian princes are obliged and subjected to this part of Moses's law, and that shall ye never be able to do, which thing we saw well enough, and therefore ye were fain to [underpin] and uphold this your ruinous and weak building, with the strong force of the law of nature. But this force, as you have heard, is but the force of a bulrush.

. . . But we will remove and relinquish all these helps, and see what and how far this authority forceth by the very words. *Frater* is the masculine gender (ye say) and therefore women are to be removed. Then by this rule women must also be excluded from their salvation, because scripture sayeth: He that shall believe and be baptized shall be saved. . . . But we will not shift your own word, *Brother.* We say therefore that this word must not be taken so straightly and narrowly as ye take it: For first not only in scripture, but in old ancient profane authors, it comprehendeth the brother's child: Yea and sometime in civil law cousin germans, coming of two brethren . . .

Again as in the civil law the masculine gender comprehendeth the feminine: So doth it in your word "brother." . . . The bequests made by the testator *fratribus,* to his brethren, shall be beneficial to his sisters also, unless it may be proved that the testator meant otherwise. Now when the Holy scripture sayeth, thou shalt not hate thy brother, thou shalt not lend upon usury to thy brother, let every man use his brother mercifully, if thy brother trespass against thee forgive him, withdraw yourselves from every brother walking disorderly, he that hateth his brother is in darkness, with a number of like suite: Shall we infer thereupon that we may hate our sister, that we may oppress our sister with usury, that we may use our sister as unmercifully as we will, without any remorse of conscience, and are not bound to forgive her, nor to eschew her company being excommunicated, or a notorious offender? Wherefore neither this word "brother" excludeth a sister, nor this word "king" in scripture excludeth a Queen: In the Greek tongue, one word representeth both brother and sister. . . . After the same rate the words "king" and "queen" are knit up in both one. . . .

Seeing then by interpretation this word "brother" containeth the word "sister" also in scripture, and the word "king" by property of one and the same voice and signification, expresseth the Queen both in scripture and in other tongues: Why should we not as well communicate to women the dignity appertaining to the name, and resembled by the same, as the name itself?

For even in this our own country, albeit the names of the king and the Queen do utterly vary one from the other, and also the ancient statutes of the realm, do not only attribute and refer all prerogative and preeminence, power and jurisdiction, unto the name of a king, but do give also, assign, and appoint the correction and punishment of all offenders, against the realm and dignity of the crown and the laws of the realm, unto the king. Yet are all manner of the aforesaid jurisdictions and other prerogatives, and ought to be, as fully, as wholly, and as absolutely in the Prince female, as in the male. And so was it ever deemed, judged and accepted, before the statute made for the farther declaration in that point.

. . . God, as long before foreseeing that there should come such unnatural cavilling quarrellers, against his creature and providence, and against their own natural princes, hath as it were all at once met with them, and answered to all such calumnious cavillings of yours and such other, as ye shall by and by understand. A woman pardie,[15] if we believe you, must not keep the state and honour of a Prince and Queen, and why so, I pray you? Was not she created to the Image of God as well as man? And doth not she represent the majesty of God? Did not God bless them both?[16] Did God not bid them rule over the fish of the sea, and over the fowl of heaven, and over every beast that moveth upon the earth? But what thing mean ye by the "Image of God"? Mean you as Saint Paul seemeth to mean? That man was created in righteousness and true holiness? This is true also in the woman. Some think that the Image of God representeth the blessed Trinity, which is (as such a high thing may be) somewhat resembled by memory, by will, and by understanding: Which are in women, as well as in men.

What thing is there that reason, wit and understanding may reach to,

---

[15] For God; a corruption of "pour Dieu."
[16] Adam and Eve.

that woman hath not, or may not achieve and attain? For learning, there have been many women exactly learned in music, astronomy, philosophy, oratory, physics, in poetry, in law and divinity. . . .

I speak it to this purpose only: To show that a woman may not only have civil regiment in other things, but may intermeddle also when the case requireth with warlike matters, and be present with the army in the field. And this also among other ancient and solemn ceremonies, the girding of our sovereign at her coronation with a sword, the setting of a pair of spurs to her heels may well signify. . . .

And so I trust ye are or have cause to be fully satisfied, as well touching your allegation that womanly regiment is against nature, as also touching a brother to be chosen king. And therefore I conclude against you, that neither the law of God, nor of nature, nor yet reason, upon which also you ground yourself, do reject the said Queen Marie from succession of the crown of England. Your reason is, that where the people erect themselves an head of their own kindred and nation, there nature assureth the people of natural government. And where a stranger carrieth opinion of unnatural tyranny, it assureth the ruler of natural subjection. To a stranger is murmur and rebellion threatened.

But now if this excellent Lady and Princess be no stranger, and be of our own kindred, and of the ancient and late royal blood of this realm (as we have declared), then is your reason also withal avoided, which may and doth oftentimes take place in more strangers, coming in by violent and forcible means. But here as natural a man as ye make yourself, ye seem to go altogether against reason and against nature also. . . .

Surely it is no more unnatural to such a Prince [as Mary Stuart] descending from the ancient and late royal blood of the kings of England, to bear rule in England, and as it were to return to the head and fountain from whence originally she sprang than it is for all floods and rivers, (which as Homer sayeth) flow out of the great ocean sea, to revert, return, and reflow again to the said ocean. This coherence, conjunction, copulation, inclination and favour running interchangeably, betwixt such a Prince and the people, is no more strange to nature, than is the conjunction of the tree and the root thereof, than of the fountain and the river issuing from thence, than of the sun, and the sunbeams; and finally, than is the conjunction betwixt the old ancient loving grandmother and her young and tender daughter.

Neither do I well know how I may better call noble England, than a loving grandmother to this good, gentle Lady whom we (I do not doubt, if ever God call her to the royal seat thereof) shall not only find a loving and gracious mistress, but a most dear and tender good daughter. . . .

If this conjunction [of England and Mary as its queen] once happen, and if we be once united and knit together in one kingdom and dominion, in one entire brotherly love and amity, as we are already knit by neighbourhood, by tongue, and almost by all manners, fashions, and behaviour, then will all unnatural and butcherly slaughter, so long hitherto practiced, cease. Then will rest, quietness, wealth, and prosperity increase at home. Then will all outward Princes, our friends, rejoice and be comforted: and our enemies dread us. Then will the honour, fame and majesty of the island of Albion daily grow more and more, and her power and strength so greatly increase, as to the friend it will be a good shield: And to the enemy a horrible terror. Then shall the outward enemy little endomage[17] us. Then shall we with our children after us, reap the pleasant fruits of this noble conjunction. . . .

4

MARY STUART AND ELIZABETH TUDOR

Letters

1569–1587

Though Mary Stuart and Elizabeth Tudor exchanged several letters during Mary's personal rule in Scotland, their correspondence became extraordinarily poignant and intense in the course of that queen's nineteen-year captivity on English soil. As we might expect, Mary wrote to Elizabeth more often than the Tudor queen wrote to her. But while it would seem obvious that Elizabeth had the upper hand in their relationship, the letters between the two actually register — even enact — a more complex and intricate struggle for power. Elizabeth's tone, although frequently imperious, is often plagued with guilt and uncertainty. Mary complains bitterly of the ransacking of her possessions and constant "bodily fear" and begs Elizabeth not to "leave me to waste away here in tears and complaints." But she also seems confident of her own ability to play upon Elizabeth's sympathies and sense of obligation to her.

[17]Damage.

G. B. Harrison, ed. *The Letters of Queen Elizabeth I* (London: Cassell, 1968). *Calendar of State Papers Relating to Scotland and Mary Queen of Scots*, ed. J. Bain, et al. (Edinburgh, 1898–1969).

Mary's tone varies dramatically, ranging from frustration to forbearance even within a single letter. All her letters convey the experience of captivity and physical suffering with extraordinary directness. Her early letters (like the one from Tutbury Castle of October 1, 1569) stress her "friendship and desire to please" Elizabeth; later correspondences (e.g., October 16, 1570) more aggressively seek to "prove my affection to you" and sometimes sound like love letters as they promise to "devote myself more and more to love, honour and obey you." Mary often petitions for "the favour of [Elizabeth's] presence," and her letter of October 29, 1571, shows her beginning to fashion herself as a Catholic martyr. She even invokes another Mary—mother of Christ—when she casts herself as a "desolate mother" deprived of her son.

Elizabeth, for her part, mistrusted Mary's letters and tried to steel herself against what she saw as their manipulative rhetoric of kinship and good will. Her letter to Mary just after the death of Darnley (dated February 24, 1567) voices both condescension and horror as Elizabeth "urge[s] you to preserve your honour." Later letters—like that of February 1, 1572—express annoyance, reprimand Mary for her "uncomely, passionate, ireful and vindictive speeches," and are laden with hauteur. Yet the careful reader will also notice that Elizabeth often imagines herself in the position of the defendant, and Mary in that of the aggressor. This reversal of apparent roles is especially evident in Elizabeth's last letter to Mary, just before her trial in October 1586, in which she accuses the Queen of Scots of having "in various ways and manners attempted to take my life and to bring my kingdom to destruction by bloodshed." Elizabeth's conviction of her own danger also shades the letters she wrote to Mary's son, James, after sentencing his mother to death: "Do I not make myself, trow ye, a goodly prey for every wretch to devour?"

However complex their epistolary game of cat and mouse might have been, and however various the roles the two queens might have assumed as they played that game, Elizabeth's announcement of Mary's death sentence in early December 1586 put a stop to it. Mary's last letter to Elizabeth, of December 19, is at last resigned. The themes of earlier letters are still present, but transmuted; the queen who once tried to prove her love now asks Elizabeth only to "see the truth of all after my death." Mary still voices her desires, but they are now simple—to be buried in France (the request was denied) and to assure that her faithful servants be well-treated after her death. The Queen of Scots still mentions her "consanguinity" with Elizabeth, but not in order to win freedom.

Elizabeth and Mary corresponded in French, but even in translation their letters reveal the tragic complexity of the ties of mistrust and obligation, identification and enmity, that bound them together.

[*Mary was moved among many castles during her long captivity. Early on, she wrote to Elizabeth protesting against her abrupt and often violent treatment.*]

FROM TUTBURY,[1] THE 1ST OCTOBER, 1569

MADAM, MY GOOD SISTER,—Perceiving by a suspicion taken of me, my sudden removal and change of keepers, and treatment of my servants, at the time when I hoped, according to your promises, to receive your favourable determination in my affairs, I could only lament that my confidence in you, and my friendship and desire to please you, have brought me a result so unhoped for and evil, in reward for my long forbearance: which always thinking to remedy by displaying to you the sincerity of my intention in all my actions towards you, I had requested permission to write to you by one of my faithful servants, in the hope that when you knew my innocence you would treat me differently. But that was refused to me; which has made me venture to send to the Bishop of Ross,[2] to give him this charge. But now seeing the severity increased, so as to compel me to dismiss my poor servants without giving them the means of going where out of respect of me they might have their livelihood, but to force them to throw themselves into the hands of the rebels, to be hanged; leaving me only twenty men, unless I choose to dismiss my women without knowing whither, without money or protection, so far from their country and in such a season; by which number it is impossible for me to be served, for the reasons which the Bishop of Ross will explain to whom you please;—that appeared to me far more severe than I ever would have expected from you: and farther, the more grievous prohibition, that I may receive no letter or message, nor intelligence of my affairs in Scotland, which are in such extremity from my having waited for your promise of having them briefly dispatched: nor even is it allowed me to hear of those in France, or of the health of the princes my friends or kinsmen, who rely, as I have done, upon your favour towards me. Instead of which, they have forbid me to go out, and have rifled my trunks, entering my chamber with pistols and arms, not without putting me in bodily fear, and accusing my people, rifle them and place them under arrest; still I should have thought that in all this finding nothing which could affect or displease you, I should thereafter have experienced better treatment. But seeing that such is the life I lead, with the prospect of its being worse, I presume to address to you this last request, containing the following:

First, that if you do not find the statement of the Bishop of Ross satisfactory, you will permit me to satisfy you in person. Secondly, that you

---

[1]The Staffordshire castle where Mary was abruptly sent after her first trial.
[2]John Leslie, Mary's Catholic advocate throughout her captivity.

will be pleased, without longer putting me off for the sake of others, to restore me to my own country and authority by your support, or to permit me, according to my former request, to retire to France to the Most Christian King my brother-in-law:[3] or, at least, that during my imprisonment I may have liberty to communicate with the Bishop of Ross and other ministers necessary to settle my affairs; and that to these my affectionate requests you will send a reply, either by one of my own people, or by letter from yourself.

And lastly, if you please to detain me your prisoner, I entreat you at least to put a ransom[4] upon me, and not leave me to waste away here in tears and complaints caused by the disease for which I came to seek the remedy. But if it please you to use me harshly without my having deserved it, at least let me not be placed in the hands of any one suspicious to my friends and relations, for fear of false reports, or worse than I should wish to think of any one.

And hoping that you will consider these my complaints and requests according to conscience, justice, your laws, your honour, and the satisfaction of all Christian princes, I shall pray God to give you a happy and long life, and me a better share in your favour than to my sorrow I perceive that I have, whereto I shall commend myself affectionately to the end.

> From my prison at Tutbury, this 1st of October
> Your very affectionate distressed sister and cousin,
> MARIE.

[During the Northern Rebellion of 1569, several lords in the north of England, many of them Catholic, mounted a disorganized uprising against Elizabeth Tudor. They acted in the name of the captive Mary Queen of Scots, who had knowledge of their plans. Mary often wrote to Elizabeth during this time, no doubt fearing blame and asserting her "humble submission and obedience."]

FROM CHATSWORTH,[5] THE 16TH OCTOBER, 1570

MADAM, MY GOOD SISTER, — I have received the letters which you were pleased to write to me by Mr. Cecil your secretary,[6] and Mr. Mildmay the chancellor of your exchequer,[7] which have produced in me two contrary effects; the one of displeasure to see by them your mistrust of my sincere

---

[3] Henri III of France, brother of Mary's first husband, François II.
[4] Mary wants Elizabeth to name a sum of money which might be paid, presumably by another monarch, to set her free.
[5] Castle on the English moors, where Mary was kept after the Ridolfi Conspiracy.
[6] Sir William Cecil, Elizabeth's Secretary of State.
[7] Sir Walter Mildmay, Chancellor of the Exchequer.

intentions, and the other of pleasure that your long silence is broken by your letters aforesaid, and your mind so far laid open by them that inasmuch as you have been pleased to instruct your trusty councillors to communicate with me on your part, I have some little room to hope, instead of despair, for some good and speedy determination of my affairs, so long expected by me; in which hope I am much confirmed in that you have been pleased to send to me two of your most agreeable and faithful councillors. From whom having learned your pleasure, and such particulars as you charged them to communicate to me, I have so freely discussed with them every point, that I trust it will satisfy you, and prove my affection to you, that on my part there remains no longer any scruple to obstruct our sincere and reciprocal friendship, which I prefer to that of any other prince. In proof of which I consent to place in your hands the most valued jewel which God has given me in this world, and my sole comfort, — my only and dear son; whose education, desired by several, is entrusted to you, and by him and me preferred before all others to your good pleasure. According to which I have willingly agreed to all obligations reasonably required, the more readily so that my intention is sincere to observe the conditions agreed upon between us, resolving henceforward to cast anchor and terminate my weary voyaging in the haven of your natural good will towards me. Having recourse, instead of a pledge, to the merit of my humble submission and obedience, which I offer to you as if I had the honour of being your daughter, as I have that of being your sister and nearest cousin, and yielding to none in obeying and honouring you now as heretofore, if you please to accept me as entirely yours. In return for which I respectfully desire the favour of your presence, which will afford indubitable assurance of your perpetual favour henceforward, and hope to induce me never to swerve from your pleasure and command. And although by your letters and messages I can depend upon your goodwill and favour, nevertheless the favour of your presence and your own word alone can stop the mouths of all those who either may vilify or try to break our treaty, esteeming it defective as wanting such an evidence of good faith between us. For how are they to judge of us, seeing that we agree in all other points, and that I have been more than two years in your power, if I return without obtaining admission to your presence; except that there is some deep-rooted displeasure in your heart towards me, seeing a similar refusal has never been made to any sovereign, so far from between a relative so near, and one who is so desirous to please you?

Then, Madam my good sister, do not refuse this my very humble request to see you before my departure, so as to remove from me all fear of being undeservedly in your disfavour; and thus, relying altogether on your goodwill, I shall have an indissoluble bond of friendship between us twain sufficient to shut the mouths of our mutual enemies who might pretend to the contrary; and, by the same means, I shall discover to you the secrets of my heart, of which I have given some insight, but darkly, to Mr. Cecil your secretary; reserving, however, the chief point to that truly happy day so much desired by me, with the deference which I begged him to communicate to you on my behalf. Hoping that, having heard from your two trusty councillors and my ambassador, whom I send to you with them hourly to receive your good pleasure and contentment, the sincerity with which I desire to proceed to satisfy you on all points, you will accede to my affectionate request. I shall devote myself more and more to love, honour, and obey you, which I am resolved to do nevertheless; and, if you please so to favour me, I would beg of you first of all to command me when you please, where you please, in what company, to remain as secretly, as long or as short, without seeing or being seen but by you, with whom alone I have to do; of which God is my witness that I have no other design but to convince you, and assure myself of your favour without prejudice to any one, but to your satisfaction and my great consolation, which I desire after God from you. Whom I pray to move your heart to receive graciously the offer which I make of mine, and that he may give you, Madam my good sister, a long and very happy life.

From Chatsworth, the 16th of October, 1570

[*After the Ridolfi Conspiracy was exposed, and with the Northern Rebellion under way, Elizabeth had Mary placed under the strictest confinement. Mary wrote to protest against such "extreme severity."*]

FROM SHEFFIELD,[8] THE 29TH OCTOBER, 1571

MADAM,—The extreme severity with which by your orders I am used, so convinces me, to my great regret, of the misfortune which I have, with many others, not only of being in your disfavour, but, which is worse, esteemed by you as an enemy instead of a friend, as a stranger instead of a relative,—even the more detested that it does not permit the exercise of Christian charity between parties so nearly related by blood and propinquity,—that for some time past I have felt so perplexed as to hesitate whether I should write to you or not; and until this moment have rather chosen to be silent than by my pen to offend you further, seeing the small estimation in which you have hitherto held my letters, and that every

---

[8]Castle in Derbyshire. Another of Mary's prisons.

thing proceeding from me offends you, as you put the worst construction upon all my actions. But at length, considering in my own mind that God proves his own by affliction, and my conscience bearing a good testimony of my conduct towards you, after thanking God for all which it pleases Him to send me, I am resolved to make Him the sole judge of my thoughts, and in all things to put my confidence in Him who never forsakes those who have rested their hopes in Him. In which having experienced great consolation, and such as keeps me secure in His mercy, and in my integrity and confidence in Him, I am emboldened to write to you the present, to unburden my heart, wherein it testifies that I have acquitted myself according to my power in the extremity in which I see myself placed by the malice of those who, without occasion for hating me, have for a long while given proof of their inclination by injuring me in your opinion and that of all others. But now, without further annoying you with the sad and pathetic complaint of an afflicted queen prisoner, I shall venture to address to you this humble and perhaps last request, that you will please for once to give me leave to confer with some one of my people from France; or, if that is not agreeable to you, with some of the attendants of M. de La Mothe, the ambassador from his most Christian Majesty, my good brother, if you do not choose that he himself should take that trouble, in order to an arrangement of my affairs in France, as well for the remuneration of my old servants now banished from my presence, as for the small number now left to me, I know not for how long, and also for the payment of my debts, which, without seeing my accounts, I am unable to discharge according to the duties of my conscience, of which I implore you to have consideration. Although I do not wish to trouble you with what concerns my condition, which, knowing to be of so little consequence to you, I leave to the mercy of God, resolved to live patiently in adversity and prison as miserable as He pleases, and to die in like manner when it shall be His will to deliver me from this wicked world; in which not knowing how long it is His pleasure that I remain, being afflicted with a disease occasioned by so many unaccustomed inconveniences or by your unmerited severity; yet I will pray you also (impelled to this by the zeal of my conscience) to permit me to have a priest of the Catholic Church, of which I am a member, to console me and attend to my duties. Which requests being granted, I shall pray God, both in prison and in dying, to give to your heart what may be agreeable to Him and wholesome for you; and if I am refused them, I charge you to answer before God for my failure in the means of doing my duty, having duly implored and requested you, in whom lies the refusal or permission.

There remains still another request, of little importance to you, but of extreme consolation to me; it is that you will please, having compassion on a desolate mother, from whose arms has been torn her only child[9] and hope of future joy in this world, to permit me to write at least open letters, to enquire into the real state of his welfare, and recall to him his sad mother; so that, receiving some comfort from his good behaviour, I may also remind him of his duty towards God and me, without which no human favour can profit him; for failing in one of these two so express commandments, God may make him forgetful of all the others. And if the above points are granted to me, I shall prepare myself at once to receive life or death, or whatsoever it may please God to send me at your hands; which having kissed, I shall conclude by praying God to give you, Madam, His holy grace in this world, and His glory in the other.

> From my close prison of Sheffield, this 29th October
> Your very good sister and cousin,
> MARIE R.

[*Mary's last letter to Elizabeth was written on December 19, 1586, after Elizabeth had proclaimed the sentence of death against her.*]

. . . And then I know that you, more than any other, ought to be touched to the heart by the honour or dishonour of your race, and of a queen, the daughter of a king. Then, madam, by the honour of Jesus—under whose name all powers obey—I require you to permit, after my enemies shall have satisfied their desire for my innocent blood, that my poor desolate servants all together may carry away my body to be buried in holy ground, and with some of my predecessors who are in France, especially the late queen my mother; and this in consideration that in Scotland the bodies of the kings my predecessors have been outraged, and the churches thrown down and profaned, and that, suffering in this country, I cannot have place by your predecessors, who are mine: and what is more, according to our religion, we set great store by being interred in holy ground.

And since I have been told that you do not wish in anything to force my conscience against my religion, and that you have even granted me a priest, I hope that you will not refuse me this last request, permitting at least free burial to the body from which the soul will have been severed, since being united they have never been able to obtain liberty to live in peace while procuring it for yourself. For which before God I give

[9]Mary here refers to her son, James VI of Scotland, from whom she had been separated for four years.

you no blame: but may God cause you to see the truth of all after my death. And because also I fear the secret tyranny of some, I pray you not to permit that my execution take place without your knowledge; not for fear of the torment, which I am very ready to suffer, but for the rumour that would be spread about my death, without witnesses not suspected; which has been done, as I am persuaded, about others of different rank. To avoid which I require that my servants may remain spectators and witnesses of my end in the faith of my Saviour and the obedience of His church; and that all together carrying away my body, as secretly as it shall please you, they may withdraw themselves without there being taken from them either their movable goods nor that which is dying I may leave them, which is very little for their good services. A jewel which I received from you I shall send back to you with my last words, or sooner if it please you. I entreat you again, and require you in the name of Jesus Christ, out of respect for our consanguinity, and for the sake of King Henry the seventh, your ancestor and mine, and by the honour of the dignity which we have held and of the sex common between us, that my request may be granted to me. For the rest I think you will well have known that in your name my canopy has been taken down,[10] and afterwards I was told that it was not by your command, but by the advice of some of the council: I praise God for such cruelty, it serving only to wreak malice, and to afflict me after having made up my mind to death; I fear that there may be many other such things. . . .

[*Elizabeth wrote to Mary shortly after the murder of Mary's husband, Lord Darnley.*]

FEBRUARY 24, 1567

MADAM,

My ears have been so astounded and my heart so frightened to hear of the horrible and abominable murder of your husband and my own cousin that I have scarcely spirit to write: Yet I cannot conceal that I grieve more for you than him. I should not do the office of a faithful cousin and friend, if I did not urge you to preserve your honour, rather than look through your fingers at revenge on those who have done you that pleasure as most people say. I counsel you so to take this matter to heart, that you may show the world what a noble Princess and loyal woman you are. I write thus vehemently not that I doubt, but for affection. . . .

---

[10]Mary's "canopy" is her cloth of state, which would have hung above her chair, and to which she clung throughout her captivity.

[*After Mary had fled Scotland, and been inconclusively tried in England for her alleged crimes against her second husband, Darnley, Elizabeth wrote to probe Mary about her role in the matter.*]

HAMPTON COURT, DECEMBER 21, 1568

MADAM,

Whilst your cause hath been here treated upon we thought it not needful to write anything thereof unto you, supposing always that your Commissioners would advertise as they saw cause. And now sithence[11] they have broken this conference by refusing to make answer as they say by your commandment, and for that purpose they return to you. Although we think you shall by them perceive the whole proceedings, yet we cannot but let you understand by these our letters, that as we have been very sorry of long time for your mishaps and great troubles, so find we our sorrows now double in beholding such things as are produced to prove yourself cause of all the same; and our grief herein is also increased in that we did not think at any time to have seen or heard such matters of so great appearance and moment to charge and condemn you. Nevertheless both in friendship, nature, and justice, we are moved to cover these matters, and stay our judgement, and not to gather any sense thereof to your prejudice before we may hear of your direct answer thereunto, according as your Commissioners understand our meaning to be: which at their request is delivered to them in writing. And as we trust they will advise you for your honour to agree to make answer as we have motioned them; so surely we cannot but as one Prince and near cousin regarding another, most earnestly as we may in terms of friendship require and charge you not to forbear from answering. And for our part, as we are heartily sorry and dismayed to find such matter of your charge, so shall we be as heartily glad and well content to bear of sufficient matter for your discharge. And although we doubt not, but you are well certified of the diligence and care of your ministers having your commission; yet can we not, beside an allowance generally of them, specially note to you, your good choice of this bearer the Bishop of Ross, who hath not only faithfully and wisely, but also carefully and dutifully for your honour and weal behaved himself and that both privately and publicly, as we cannot but in this sort commend him unto you, as we wish you had many such devoted discreet servants. For in our judgement, we think ye have not any that in loyalty and faithfulness can overmatch him. And this we

---

[11] Since.

are the bolder to write, considering we take it the best trial of a good servant to be in adversity, out of which we wish you to be delivered by the justification of your innocency. And so trusting to hear shortly from you, we make an end.

[*Mary had been gravely ill and, fearful that she would die, willed her claim to the English crown, as well as her rights in Scotland, to her brother-in-law, the French King Henri III, and his heirs. Elizabeth, alarmed, wrote to the Queen of Scots during her convalescence.*]

MAY 25, 1569

MADAM,
To my infinite regret I have learned the great danger in which you have lately been; and I praise God that I heard nothing of it until the worst was past, for in whatever time or place it might have been, such news could have given me little content; but if any such bad accident had befallen you in this country, I believe really I should have deemed my days prolonged too long, if previous to death I had received such a wound. I rely much on His goodness Who has always guarded me against such mal-accidents, that He will not permit me to fall into such a snare, and that He will preserve me in the good report of the world till the end of my career. He has made me know, by your means, the grief I might have felt if anything ill had happened to you, and I assure you that I will offer up to Him infinite thanksgivings.

As to the reply that you wish to receive by my Lord Boyd,[12] regarding my satisfaction in the case touching the Duke of Anjou,[13] I neither doubt your honour nor your faith in writing to me that you never thought of such a thing, but that perhaps some relative, or rather some Ambassador of yours, having the general authority of your signature to order all things for the furtherance of your affairs, had adjusted this promise as if it came from you, and deemed it within the range of his commission. Such a matter would serve as a spur to a courser of high mettle; for, as we often see a little bough serve to save the life of a swimmer, so a light shadow of claim animates the combatants. I know not why they[14] consider not that the bark of your good fortune floats on a dangerous sea, where many contrary winds blow, and has need of all aid to obviate such evils and to conduct you safely into port.

---

[12]Emissary between Elizabeth and Mary.
[13]There was a possibility at this time that Elizabeth might marry the Duke of Anjou— a deeply alarming prospect to many of her subjects.
[14]The royal family of France.

[*After the Ridolfi Conspiracy against Elizabeth was discovered, the guard around the Queen of Scots was tightened severely. Mary protested in a series of angry letters. Elizabeth aimed to ignore them but Mary's "ireful and vindictive" tone at last pushed her to reply.*]

WESTMINSTER, FEBRUARY 1, 1572

MADAME,

Of late time I have received divers letters from you, to the which you may well guess by the accidents of the time why I have not made any answer, but especially because I saw no matter in them that required any such answer as could have contented you; and to have discontented you had been but an increase of your impatience, which I thought time would have mitigated as it commonly does when the cause thereof is not truly grounded, and that it be so understood. But now finding by your last letter of the 27th of the last an increase of your impatience, tending also to uncomely, passionate, ireful and vindictive speeches, I thought to change my former opinion, and by patient and advised words to move you to stay or qualify your passions, and to consider that it is not the manner to obtain good things with evil speeches, nor benefits with injurious challenges, nor to conclude, all in one word, good to yourself, with doing evil to myself. Yet to avoid the fault which I note that you have committed in filling a long letter with multitude of sharp and injurious words, I will not by way of letter write any more of the matter, but have rather chosen to commit to my cousin, the Earl of Shrewsbury, the things which I have thought meet, upon the reading of your letter, to be imparted to you, as he hath in a memorial in writing to show to you; wherewith, I think, if reason may be admitted to be with you at the reading, you will follow hereafter the course of the last part of your letter rather than the first (the latter being written in a calm, and the former in a storm), wishing to you the same grace of God that we wish to ourself, and that He may direct you to desire and attain to that is meet for you as well in honour as in all other quietness.

[*Elizabeth wrote Mary a personal letter shortly before the trial of the Queen of Scots began.*]

OCTOBER 1586

You have in various ways and manners attempted to take my life and to bring my kingdom to destruction by bloodshed. I have never proceeded so harshly against you, but have, on the contrary, protected and maintained you like myself. These treasons will be proved to you and all made manifest. Yet it is my will, that you answer the nobles and peers of the kingdom as if I were myself present. I therefore require, charge, and command that you make answer for I have been well informed of your arrogance.

Act plainly without reserve, and you will sooner be able to obtain favour of me.

ELIZABETH

[*After Elizabeth had signed Mary's proclamation of death—but before she had signed her death warrant—she sent a letter to Mary's son, James VI of Scotland, attempting to explain her actions.*]

JANUARY 1587

I find myself so troubled lest sinister tales might delude you, my good brother, that I have willingly found out this messenger, whom I know most sincere to you and a true subject to me, to carry unto you my most sincere meaning toward you, and to request this just desire, that you never doubt my entire goodwill in your behalf; and do protest, that, if you knew, even since the arrival of your Commissioners (which if they liest, they may tell you), the extreme danger my life was in, by an Ambassador's honest silence, if not invention, and such good complices as have themselves, by God's permission, unfolded the whole conspiracy, and have avouched it before his face, though it be the peril of their own lives, yet voluntarily, one of them never being suspected brake it with a Councillor to make me acquainted therewith. You may see whither I keep the serpent that poisons me, when they confess to have reward. By saving of her life they would have had mine. Do I not make myself, trow ye, a goodly prey for every wretch to devour? Transfigure yourself into my state, and suppose what you ought to do, and thereafter weigh my life, and reject the care of murder, and shun all baits that may untie our amities, and let all men know, that Princes know best their own laws, and misjudge not that you know not. For my part, I will not live to wrong the meanest. And so I conclude you with your own words, you will prosecute or mislike as much those that seek my ruin as if they sought your heart blood, and would I had none in mine if I would not do the like; as God knoweth, to Whom I make my humble prayers to inspire you with best desires.

Your most affectionate sister and cousin,
ELIZABETH R.

I am sending you a gentleman forthwith, the other being fallen sick, who I trust shall yield you good reason of my actions.

5

The Bond of Association

1584

In the fall of 1584, two years before Mary Stuart came to trial for treason, Elizabeth's Privy Council—led by her Secretary of State, Francis Walsingham— drafted the so-called Bond of Association. The document was essentially a written oath that was signed by thousands of (male) English subjects; it quickly passed into law as the Act of Association. Its signatories bound themselves to "love, fear, and obey" their queen; such love, fear, and obedience in turn created the obligation to avenge her against the perpetrator of any "wicked attempt against her most royal person," regardless of whether that perpetrator was of royal blood.

The Bond was composed—and signed—with Elizabeth's most celebrated enemy, Mary Queen of Scots, in mind, and, without naming Mary outright, it specified that anyone who took Elizabeth's life, or even "procured" its taking, could never later succeed to the English throne. As Elizabeth's subjects committed themselves "never to allow, accept or favour any such pretended successor," they gave themselves a role in determining the direction of their own monarchy; they also took an active part in the course of justice.

Besides paving the way to Mary Stuart's trial and punishment, the Bond documents the birth of a collective identity, one formed around a common love object—Elizabeth Tudor—and against a common enemy, Mary Queen of Scots.

Forasmuch as Almighty God hath ordained Kings, Queens, and Princes to have dominion and rule over all their subjects, and to preserve them in the possession and observation of the true Christian religion, according to His holy word and commandment; and in like sort, that all subjects should love, fear, and obey their sovereign princes, being kings or queens, to the utmost of their power; at all times to withstand, pursue, and suppress all manner of persons, that shall by any means intend and attempt any thing dangerous or hurtful to the honour, state, or persons of their sovereigns. Therefore, we whose names are or shall be subscribed to this writing, being natural-born subjects of this realm of England; and having so gracious a lady, our sovereign Elizabeth by the ordinance of God, our

most rightful Queen, reigning over us these many years with great felicity, to our inestimable comfort; and finding lately by divers depositions,
confessions, and sundry advertisements out of foreign parts, from credible persons well known to her majesty's council, and to divers others, that
for the furtherance and advancement of some pretended title to the crown,
it hath been manifested, that the life of our gracious sovereign Queen Elizabeth hath been most dangerously designed against, to the peril of her
person, if Almighty God, her perpetual defender, of His mercy had not
revealed and withstood the same; by whose life, we, and all other her
majesty's true and loyal subjects, do enjoy all inestimable benefit of peace
in this land: do for these reasons and causes before alledged, not only
acknowledge ourselves most justly bound with our lives and goods for her
defence, and in her safety to prosecute, suppress and withstand all such
intenders, and all other her enemies, of what nation, condition or degree
soever they shall be, or by what counsel or title they shall pretend to be
her enemies, or to attempt any harm upon her person; but do further think
it our bounden duties, for the great benefit of peace, wealth, and godly government, we have more plentifully received these many years under her
majesty's government, than any of our forefathers have done in any longer
time of any of her progenitors, kings of this realm; to declare, and by this
writing make manifest our bounden duties to our sovereign lady for her
safety. And to that end, we and every of us, first calling to witness the name
of Almighty God, do voluntarily and most willingly bind ourselves, every
one of us to the other, jointly and severally in the band of one firm and
loyal society; and do hereby vow and promise by the majesty of Almighty
God, that with our whole powers, bodies, lives and goods, and with our
children and servants, we and every of us will faithfully serve, and humbly
obey our said sovereign lady Queen Elizabeth, against all states, dignities
and earthly powers whatsoever; and will as well with our joint and particular forces during our lives withstand, pursue and offend, as well by force
of arms, as by all other means of revenge, all manner of persons, of whatsoever state they shall be, and their abettors, that shall attempt any act,
or counsel or consent to any thing that shall tend to the harm of her
majesty's royal person; and will never desist from all manner of forcible
pursuit against such persons, to the utter extermination of them, their
counsellors, aiders and abettors. And if any such wicked attempt against
her most royal person shall be taken in hand, or procured, whereby any
that have, may or shall pretend title to come to this crown by the untimely
death of her majesty so wickedly procured (which God of His mercy forbid!) that the same may be avenged, we do not only bind ourselves both
jointly and severally never to allow, accept or favour any such pretended
successor, by whom or for whom any such detestable act shall be

attempted or committed, as unworthy of all government in any Christian realm or civil state. But do also further vow and protest, as we are most bound, and that in the presence of the eternal and everlasting God, to prosecute such person or persons to death, with our joint and particular forces, and to act the utmost revenge upon them, that by any means we or any of us can devise and do, or cause to be devised and done for their utter overthrow and extirpation. And to the better corroboration of this our Loyal Band and Association, we do also testify by this writing, that we do confirm the contents hereof by our oaths corporally taken upon the holy evangelists, with this express condition. That no one of us shall for any respect of person or causes, or for fear or reward, separate ourselves from this association, or fail in the prosecution thereof during our lives, upon pain of being by the rest of us prosecuted and supprest as perjured persons, and as public enemies to God, our queen, and to our native country; to which punishment and pains we do voluntarily submit ourselves, and every of us, without benefit of any colour and pretence. In witness of all which premises to be inviolably kept, we do to this writing put our hands and seals; and shall be most ready to accept and admit any others hereafter to this Society and Association.

6

Record of the State Trial of Mary Queen of Scots

1586

In May of 1585, England entered a series of military confrontations with Spain; anti-Catholic fever immediately set in at home. As the fever mounted, fear grew that English Catholics might rise up against the Tudor government, presumably in the name of the captive Catholic queen (and claimant to the English crown), Mary Stuart. As if on cue, a plot to kill Elizabeth Tudor and put Mary on the throne was indeed hatched through the joint efforts of an English priest, John Ballard, and a young English Catholic, Anthony Babington, among others. Walsingham nudged the conspiracy along in hopes of incriminating the participants and eventually Mary Stuart herself. Mary did her part by beginning a secret correspondence with

William Cobbett, ed. *Cobbett's Parliamentary History of England* (London: R. Bagshaw, 1806–1812).

Babington, which Walsingham closely monitored. On August 2, 1586, Babington was arrested and soon he had confessed to having communicated his plans to the Queen of Scots. Mary's own secretaries, Gilbert Curle and Claude Nau, testified that she was indeed the author of several conspiratorial letters to Babington, and she was brought to trial for treason against Elizabeth and the English state.

The proceedings against the Queen of Scots began on October 15, 1586, and ended the following day. At Elizabeth's request, they took place at Fotheringay Castle, in the county of Northamptonshire. The trial scene was stark and spare: At the upper end of Fotheringay's great room stood an empty chair draped with the cloth of state to represent the absent Elizabeth; Mary's place was opposite, with onlookers grouped behind her. The examining commission sat divided along the side walls, and included thirty-six peers, judges, and members of Elizabeth's Privy Council, all appointed by the Tudor queen, and only two of them sharing Mary's Catholic religion.

Like all accused traitors, Mary was denied counsel. Forced to defend herself, she rose to the occasion despite her lack of familiarity with both English law and the English language, and despite being allowed to make only brief notes concerning the charges against her. The American reader of today should realize that at Mary's trial there was no prosecuting lawyer, judge, or jury in any modern sense: The members of the English commission before whom Mary appeared acted as both prosecutors and judges.

The document that has become the definitive record of the trial comes from the notes of those present, including two official "writers." These notes were amalgamated in the early nineteenth century from the Hardwicke State Papers and the Burghley papers, among other sources, by the journalist and political activist William Cobbett, as part of his authoritative record of England's state trials. Some of Mary's most powerful words were actually spoken to her accusers before her trial; the trial document includes them as well.

The most part of these Commissioners came the 11th of October to Fotheringay Castle, in the county of Northampton, seated upon the bank of the river Nen, where the Queen of Scots was then kept. The next day the Commissioners sent to her Sir Walter Mildmay, Paulet,[1] and Edward Barker, a public notary, who delivered into her hands Queen Elizabeth's letter, which, when she had read, she, with a countenance composed to royal dignity, and with a mind untroubled, said, "It grieveth me that the Queen, my most dear sister, is misinformed of me; and that I, having been

---

[1] Sir Amyas Paulet. Protestant owner of Fotheringay and Mary's keeper in her final ordeal.

so many years straitly kept in prison, and grown lame of my limbs, have lien[2] neglected, after I have offered so many reasonable conditions for my liberty. Though I have thoroughly forewarned her of many dangers, yet hath no credit been given unto me, but I have been always contemned, though most nearly allied unto her in blood. When the Association[3] was entered in, and the Act of Parliament thereupon made, I foresaw that whatsoever danger should happen either from foreign princes abroad, or from ill-disposed people at home, or for religion's sake, I must bear the whole blame, having many mortal enemies in the Court. Certainly I might take it hardly, and not without cause, that a Confederacy hath been made with my son without my knowledge:[4] but such matters I omit. As for this Letter, it seemeth strange to me, that the Queen should command me as a subject to appear personally in judgment. I am an absolute Queen, and will do nothing which may prejudice either mine own royal majesty, or other princes of my place and rank, or my son. My mind is not yet dejected, neither will I sink under my calamity. I refer myself to those things, which I have protested before Bromley, now Chancellor, and the Lord La-Ware. The laws and statutes of England are to me most unknown; I am destitute of counsellors, and who shall be my peers I am utterly ignorant. My Papers and Notes are taken from me, and no man dareth step forth to be my advocate. I am clear from all crime against the Queen, I have excited no man against her, and I am not to be charged but by mine own word or writing, which cannot be produced against me. Yet can I not deny but I have commended myself and my Cause to foreign princes."

The next day there returned unto her in the name of the Commissioners, Paulet and Barker, who showed unto her this Answer drawn in Writing, and asked her whether she would persist in the same. When she had heard it distinctly read she commended it as rightly and truly conceived, and said, she would persist therein. But this, said she, I have forgotten, which I would have to be added thereunto. Whereas the Queen hath written, that I am subject to the laws of England, and to be judged by them, because I have lived under the protection of them; I answer that I came into England to crave aid, and ever since have been detained in Prison, and could not enjoy the protection or benefit of the laws of England; nay, I could never yet understand from any man what manner of laws those were.

In the afternoon came unto her certain selected persons from amongst

---

[2]Lain.

[3]The Act of Association.

[4]Perhaps a reference to the Queen's Safety Act, which assured that the English crown could pass to Mary's son, James, regardless of her fate or actions.

the Commissioners, with men learned in the civil and canon law. But the Lord Chancellor and the Lord Treasurer declared their authority by patent, and shewed that neither her imprisonment nor her prerogative of royal majesty could exempt her from answering in this kingdom; with fair words advising her to hear what matters were to be objected against her: otherwise they threatened, that by authority of law, they both could and would proceed against her, though she were absent. She answered, That she was no subject, and rather would she die a thousand deaths than acknowledge herself a subject, considering that by such an acknowledgment she should both prejudice the height of regal majesty, and withal confess herself to be bound by all the laws of England, even in matter of religion: Nevertheless she was ready to answer to all things in a free and full Parliament, for that she knew not whether this meeting and assembly were appointed against her, being already condemned by forejudgings, to give some shew and colour of a just and legal proceeding. She warned them, therefore, to look to their consciences, and to remember that the theatre of the whole world is much wider than the kingdom of England. She began then to complain of injuries done unto her; and the Lord Treasurer, interrupting her, began to reckon up Queen Elizabeth's kindnesses towards her, namely, that she had punished some which impugned the claim she laid to England, and had been a means to keep her from being condemned by the estates of the realm for the marriage sought with the Duke of Norfolk, for the rebellion in the north, and for other matters. All which when she seemed little to esteem they returned back.[5]

Within few hours after they delivered unto her, by the hands of Paulet and the Solicitor, the chief points of their Commission, and the names of the Commissioners, that she might see that they were to proceed according to equity and right, and not by any cunning point of law and extraordinary course. She took no Exceptions against the Commissioners, but most sharply excepted against the late law, upon which the authority of their Commission wholly depended, as that it was unjust, devised of purpose against her, that it was without example, and such whereunto she would never subject herself. She asked, by what law they would proceed. If by the civil or canon law, then said she, interpreters are to be fetched from Pavia, or Poictiers, and other foreign Universities; for in England none are to be found that are meet. She added also, that it was manifest,

---

[5]In the early 1570s there had been prolonged negotiations for Mary to marry her English supporter, the Duke of Norfolk. The Northern Rebellion had been closely linked to this possibility, and Elizabeth had not punished Mary for her role in it.

by plain words in the Queen's Letters, That she was already forejudged to be guilty of the crime, though unheard; And therefore there was no reason why she should appear before them: And she required to be satisfied touching some scruples in the said Letters, which she had for herself noted confusedly and by snatches, severally by themselves, but would not deliver them written out; for it stood not, said she, with her royal dignity, to play the scrivener.

Touching this matter, the said selected Commissioners went unto her again, to whom she signified that she did not well understand what those words meant, "seeing she is under the Queen's protection." The Lord Chancellor answered, That this was plain to every one of understanding, yet was it not for subjects to interpret what the queen's meaning was, neither were they made Commissioners for that end. Then she required to have her protestation shewed and allowed, which she had formerly made. It was answered, that it never had been, nor now was to be allowed, for that it was prejudicial to the Crown of England. She asked, By what authority they would proceed? It was answered, by authority of their Commission, and by the common law of England.

But, said she, Ye make laws at your pleasure, whereunto I have no reason to submit myself, considering that the English in times past refused to submit themselves to the Law Salique of France; and if they would proceed by the common law of England, they should produce precedents and cases, forasmuch as that law consisteth much of cases and custom; and if by the canon law, none else ought to interpret the same, but the makers thereof. It was answered, that they would proceed neither by the Civil nor Canon law, but by the Common Law of England; that it might nevertheless be proved by the civil and canon law, that she ought to appear before them, if she would not refuse to hear it. And indeed she refused not to hear it, but, as she said, by way of *Interlocution*, not *Judicially*.

From hence she fell into other speeches, That she had intended nothing to the destruction of the queen; that she had been incensed with injuries and indignities; that she should be a stone of offence to others, if she were so unworthily handled; . . . that she would have defended her innocency by letter, but it was not allowed her; and finally, that all the offices of kindness which she had tendered these twenty years, were rejected. Thus while she wandered far in these digressions, they called her back again, and prayed her to speak plainly, whether she would answer before the Commissioners. She replied, That the authority of their delegation was founded upon a late law made to entrap her; that she could not away with the queen's laws, which she had good reason to suspect; that she was still full of good courage, and would not offend against her progenitors, the kings of Scots, by acknowledging herself a subject to the crown of England; for this were nothing else but to profess them openly to have been rebels and traitors. Yet she refused not to answer, so as she might not be reduced to the rank of a subject. But she had rather perish utterly than to answer as a criminal person.

Whereunto, Hatton, Vice-Chamberlain to Queen Elizabeth, answered. You are accused (but not condemned) to have conspired the Destruction of our lady and queen anointed. You say you are a queen; be it so. But in such a crime the royal dignity is not exempted from answering, neither by the Civil nor Canon law, nor by the Law of Nations, nor of nature. For if such kind of offences might be committed without punishment, all justice would stagger, yea, fall to the ground. If you be innocent, you wrong your reputation in avoiding a Trial. You protest yourself to be innocent, but Queen Elizabeth thinketh otherwise, and that neither without grief and sorrow for the same. To examine, therefore, your innocency, she have appointed for Commissioners most honourable, prudent and upright men, who are ready to hear you according to equity with favour, and will rejoice with all their hearts, if you shall clear yourself of this crime. Believe me, the Queen herself will be much affected with joy, who affirmed unto me at my coming from her, that never any thing befel her more grievous, than that you were charged with such a crime. Wherefore lay aside the bootless privilege of royal dignity, which now can be of no use unto you, appear in judgment, and shew your innocency, lest by avoiding Trial, you draw upon yourself suspicion, and lay upon your reputation an eternal blot and aspersion.

I refuse not (she said) to answer in a full parliament before the estates of the realm lawfully assembled, so as I may be declared the next to the succession; yea, before the Queen and Council, so as my protestation may be admitted, and I may be acknowledged the next of kin to the queen. To the judgment of mine adversaries, amongst whom I know all defence of mine innocency will be barred, flatly, I will not submit myself.

The Lord Chancellor asked her, whether she would answer, if her Protestation were admitted? I will never (said she) submit myself to the late law mentioned in the Commission.

Hereupon the Lord Treasurer answered. We, notwithstanding, will proceed to-morrow in the Cause, though you be absent and continue contumax.[6]

[6]In contempt of court.

Search (said she) your consciences, look to your honour, God reward you and yours for your Judgment against me.

On the morrow, which was the 14th of the month, she sent for certain of the Commissioners, and prayed them, that her Protestation might be admitted and allowed. The Lord Treasurer asked her, Whether she would appear to her Trial, if her Protestation were only received and put in writing, without allowance. She yielded at length, yet with much ado, and with an ill-will, lest she should seem (as she said) to derogate from her predecessors or successors; but was very desirous to purge herself of the crime objected against her, being persuaded by Hatton's reasons, which she had weighed with advisement.

Soon after, the Commissioners, which were present, assembled themselves, in the presence chamber. At the upper end of the Chamber was placed a chair of estate for the Queen of England, under a cloth of estate. Over-against it, below and more remote, near the transom or beam that ran cross the room, stood a chair for the Queen of Scots. At the walls on both sides, were placed benches, upon which sate, on the one side, the Lord Chancellor of England, Lord Treasurer of England, the Earls of Oxford, Kent, Derby, Worcester, Rutland, Cumberland, Warwick, Pembroke, Lincoln, and the Lord Viscount Montacute; on the other side the Barons of Abergavenny, Zouch, Morley, Stafford, Grey, Lumley, Sturton, Sandes, Wentworth, Mordant, St. John of Bletsho, Compton, and Cheiney. Nigh unto these sate the knights of the Privy Council, Sir James a [sic] Croftes, Sir Christopher Hatton, Sir Frances Walsingham, Sir Ralph Sadleir, Sir Walter Mildmay, and Sir Amias Powlet. Forward before the earls, sate the two Chief Justices, and the Chief Baron of the Exchequer; and on the other side two barons, the other Justices, Dale and Ford, doctors of the Civil Law; and at a little table in the midst sate Popham, the queen's Attorney; Egerton, the Solicitor; Gaudy, the queen's Sergeant at law, the clerk of the crown, and two Writers.

When she was come, and had settled herself in her seat, after silence proclaimed, Bromley, Lord Chancellor, turning to her, spake briefly to this effect. The most high and mighty Queen Elizabeth, being not without great grief of mind advertised, that you have conspired the Destruction of her and of England, and the Subversion of Religion, hath, out of her office and duty, lest she might seem to have neglected God, herself and her people, and out of no malice at all, appointed these Commissioners to hear the matters which shall be objected unto you, and how you can clear yourself of them, and make known your innocency.

She, rising up, said, That she came into England to crave aid, which had been promised her, and yet was she detained ever since in prison. She protested, that she was no subject of the queen's, but had been and was a free and absolute queen, and not to be constrained to appear before Commissioners, or any other Judge whatsoever, for any cause whatsoever, save before God alone the highest Judge, lest she should prejudice her own royal majesty, the King of Scots her son, her successors, or other absolute princes. But, that she now appeared personally, to the end to refute the crimes objected against her. And hereof she prayed her own attendants to bear witness.

The Lord Chancellor, not acknowledging that any Aid had been promised her, answered, That this Protestation was in vain, for that whosoever (of what place and degree soever he were) should offend against the laws of England, in England, was subject unto the same laws, and by the late act might be examined and tried; the said Protestation therefore made in prejudice of the laws and Queen of England, was not to be admitted. The Commissioners nevertheless commanded, that as well as her Protestation, the Lord Chancellor's Answer should be recorded.

Then after the Commission was openly read, which was grounded upon the Act already often mentioned, she stoutly opposed her Protestation against the said Act, as enacted directly and purposely against her, and herein she appealed to their consciences.

When Answer was made by the Lord Treasurer, that every person in this kingdom was bound even by the latest laws, and that she ought not to speak against the laws; and that the Commissioners would judge, according to that law, what Protestations or Appellations soever she interposed, she said at length that she was ready to hear and answer touching any fact whatsoever against the Queen of England.

Gawdy now opened the law from point to point, affirming, that she had offended against the same; and hereupon he made an historical discourse of Babington's conspiracy, and concluded, That she knew of it, approved it, assented unto it, promised her assistance, and shewed the way and means.

She answered with stout courage, that she knew not Babington, that she never received any Letters from him, nor wrote any to him; that she never plotted the destruction of the queen, and that to prove the same, her Subscription under her own hand was to be produced; that for her part she never so much as heard speak thereof; that she knew not Ballard, nor ever relieved him; but she understood from some, that the Catholics in England took many things very hardly, and hereof she herself had advertised the Queen by Letters, and besought her to take pity on them; that many also, which were to her utterly unknown, had offered her their help and assistance, yet had she excited no man to commit any offence; and being shut up in prison, she could neither know nor hinder what they attempted.

Hereupon it was urged out of Babington's Confession that there had been intercourse by Letters betwixt her and Babington. She confessed that there had passed Conference by Letters betwixt her and many men, yet could it not thereby be gathered that she was privy to all their wicked counsels. She required that her own Subscription, under her hand, might be produced; and asked what hurt it were if she re-demanded the Letters which had been kept from her almost a whole year? Then were read the copies of letters between her and Babington, wherein the whole Conspiracy was set down. . . .

As for these Letters (said she), it may be that Babington wrote them, but let it be proved that I received them. If Babington or any others affirm it, I say they lye openly; other men's crimes are not to be cast upon me. A Packet of Letters, which had been kept from me almost a whole year, came to my hands about that time, but by whom it was sent I know not.

To prove that she had received Babington's Letters, there were read out of Babington's Confession the chief heads of certain Letters, which he had voluntarily confessed, that she wrote back unto him; wherein when mention was made of the Earl of Arundel and his brethren and the Earl of Northumberland the tears burst forth and she said, Alas! what hath that noble house of the Howards endured for my sake? and shortly after, having wiped away the tears, she answered That Babington might confess what he list, but it was an open lye, that she had devised such means to escape. . . .

There were read also certain points picked out of Savage's and Ballard's Confessions,[7] who had confessed that Babington imparted unto them certain Letters which he had received from the Queen of Scots.

She affirmed, That Babington received none from her, yea, that she was angry with some which had secretly suggested counsels unto her for invading of England, and had warned them to beware. . . .

[At this point, several of the letters which had passed between Mary and Babington were read aloud.]

Of this Letter she required a Copy, and affirmed, That it proceeded not from her, but haply from her Alphabet of Ciphers[8] in France; That

---

[7]John Savage and John Ballard, two of Babington's co-conspirators. Ballard was an English Catholic priest.

[8]A secret code transferred manually to the page.

she had done her best endeavour for the recovery of her liberty, which Nature itself alloweth, and had solicited her friends to deliver her; yet to some, whom she listed not to name, when they offered her their help to deliver her, she answered not a word. Nevertheless, she much desired to divert the storm of persecution from the Catholics, and for this she had made earnest suit to the Queen: for her part, she would not purchase the kingdom with the death of the meanest man of the common people, much less of the Queen; That there were many which attempted dangerous designs without her knowledge; and by a very late Letter which she had received, Pardon was asked of her by some, if they should enterprise anything without her privity: That it was an easy matter to counterfeit the Ciphers and Characters of others, as a young man did very lately in France, which had vaunted himself to be her son's base brother: That she feared also lest this were done now by Walsingham to bring her to her death, who, as she heard, had practised against her life and her son's. She protested that she had not so much as thought the destruction of the Queen; that she had rather most gladly spend her own life than for her sake the Catholics should be so afflicted in hatred of her, and drawn to cruel death. And withal she shed plenty of tears.

But (said the Lord Treasurer) no man which hath showed himself a good subject was ever put to death for Religion; but some have been for Treason, while they maintained the Pope's Bull and authority against the Queen. Yet I, said she, have heard otherwise, and have read it also in Books set forth in print. The Authors, replied he, of such Books do write also that the Queen had forfeited her royal dignity.

Walsingham, who had found himself taxed even now by her words, took opportunity, and rising up, protested that his mind was free from all malice; I call God, said he, to record that as a private person I have done nothing unbeseeming an honest man; nor, as I bear the place of a public person, have I done anything unworthy my place. I confess that, being very careful for the safety of the Queen and realm, I have curiously searched out the practices against the same. If Ballard had offered me his help I should not have refused it; yea, I would have recompensed the pains he had taken. If I have practised anything with him, why did he not utter it to save his life?

With this answer she said she was satisfied: She prayed him he would not be angry that she had spoken freely what she had heard reported; and that he would give no more credit to those that slandered her than she did to such who accused him: That Spies were men of doubtful credit, which dissemble one thing and speak another; and that he would in no sort believe that she had consented to the Queen's destruction. And now, again, she burst forth into tears: I would never, said she, make shipwreck of my soul by conspiring the destruction of my dearest sister.

It was answered by the Lawyers that this should soon be disproved by Testimony. Thus far in the forenoon.

In the afternoon, to disprove this, was produced the Copy of a letter which Charles Paget had written; and Curle, one of her secretaries, had witnessed that she had received; touching a Conference betwixt Mendoza[9] and Ballard, about the design for invading of England and setting her at liberty. This, answered she, was nothing to the purpose, and proved not that she had consented to the destruction of the Queen.

The Lawyers proceeded further to prove that she was both privy to the Conspiracy, and conspired also the Destruction of the Queen, by Babington's Confession, and Letters also that had passed betwixt her and him; wherein he called her his most dread and sovereign lady and queen. And, by the way, they mentioned that a Plot was laid for conveying the kingdom of England to the Spaniard. She confessed that a priest came unto her and said, That if she would not intermeddle she and her son both should be excluded from the inheritance; but the priest's name she would not tell. She added that the Spaniard did lay claim to the kingdom of England, and would not give place to any but to her.

Then pressed they her with the Testimonies of her Secretaries, Nau and Curle, out of Babington's Confession, and the Letters sent to and fro betwixt her and Babington, and the whole credit of their Proofs rested upon their testimony; yet were not they produced before her face to face. Curle she acknowledged an honest man; but not a meet Witness to be against her. As for Nau, he had been sometimes a Secretary, said she, to the Cardinal of Lorain, and Commended unto her by the French King, and might easily be drawn either by reward, or hope, or fear, to bear false witness, as one that had sundry times rashly bound himself by oath, and had Curle so pliable unto him that at his beck he would write what he bade him. It might be that these two might insert into her Letters such things as she had not dictated unto them. It might be also that such Letters came to their hands which notwithstanding she never saw; and so she brake forth into such words as these: The majesty and safety of all princes falleth to the ground if they depend upon the Writings and Testimony of Secretaries. I delivered nothing to them but what nature delivered to me, that I might at length recover my liberty. And I am not to be

---

[9]Bernardino de Mendoza, a Spanish diplomat through whom Mary had promised to give her right to the English throne to Philip II of Spain should her Protestant son, James, not convert to the Catholic faith.

convicted but by mine own Word or Writing. If they have written anything which may be hurtful to the Queen, my sister, they have written it altogether without my knowledge; and let them bear the punishment of their inconsiderate boldness. Sure I am, if they were here present, they would clear me of all blame in this Cause. And I, if my Notes were at hand, could answer particularly to these things.

Amongst these speeches the Lord Treasurer objected unto her, that she had purposed to send her son into Spain, and to convey her Title she claimeth in the Kingdom of England to the Spaniard. To whom she answered that she had no kingdom which she could convey, yet was it lawful for her to give those things which were hers, at her pleasure, and not to be accountable for the same to any.

When her Alphabets of Ciphers, sent over to Babington, the Lord Lodouic and Fernihurst were objected unto her out of Curle's testimony; she denied not, but she had written out many; and, amongst others, that for the Lord Lodouic, when she had commended him and another to the dignity of a Cardinal; and that without offence (she trusted), for that it was as lawful for her to have intercourse of Letters and to negotiate her matters with men of her Religion as for the Queen with the professors of another religion.

Then pressed they her hard with the consenting Testimonies of Nau and Curle reiterated: And she reiterated her Answers, or else refelled[10] their Testimonies by a flat denial; protesting again that she neither knew Babington nor Ballard. . . .

The next day she returned her former Protestation, and required to have it recorded, and a Copy thereof delivered to her, lamenting that the most reasonable conditions, which she had many times propounded to the Queen, were always rejected, even when she promised to deliver her son and the Duke of Guise's son for hostages, that the Queen or Kingdom of England should receive no detriment by her, so as she saw herself already quite barred from all hope of her liberty. But now she was most unworthily dealt withal, whose honour and reputation was called in question before foreign lawyers, which by wretched conclusions drew every circumstance into a consequence; whereas princes anointed and consecrate are not subject to the same laws that private men are. Moreover, whereas authority was granted to the Commissioners to examine matters tending to the hurt of the Queen's person; yet was the Cause so handled, and Letters wrested, that the religion which she professed, the

[10]Refuted.

immunity and majesty of foreign princes, and the private intercourse betwixt princes were called in question, and she herself made to descend beneath her royal dignity, and to appear as a party guilty before a tribunal seat; and all to no other purpose but that she might be quite excluded out of the Queen's favour and her own right to the succession; whereas she appeared voluntarily to clear herself of the matters objected against her, lest she might seem to have neglected the defence of her own honour and innocency. She called also to remembrance how Queen Elizabeth herself had been drawn in question about Wyat's Conspiracy, whereas notwithstanding she was most[11] innocent; religiously affirming that though she wished the safety of the Catholics might be provided for, yet would she not that it should be effected with the death and blood of any one. For her part, she had rather play Hester than Judith, make intercession[12] to God for the people, than deprive the meanest of the people of life. She expostulated, that her enemies had divulged abroad that she was irreligious; but the time was (said she) when I would have been instructed in the Protestant Religion, but they would not suffer me to be so, as if they cared not what became of my soul. And now, concluding, When ye have done all ye can (said she) against me, and have excluded me from my right, ye may chance fail of your cause and hope. And withal making her appeal to God, and to the princes, her kinsmen, and renewing her Protestation, she prayed that there might be another meeting about this matter, and that an advocate might be granted unto her to plead her Cause, and that, seeing she was a princess, she might be believed in the word of a princess: For it were extreme folly to stand to their judgment whom she saw most plainly to be armed with prejudice against her.

To these things the Lord Treasurer said. Whereas I bear a double person, one of a Commissioner, another of a Counsellor, receive first a few words from me as a Commissioner. Your Protestation is recorded, and a Copy thereof shall be delivered unto you. To us our authority is granted under the Queen's hand, and the great seal of England, from which there is no appeal; neither do we come with prejudice, but to judge according to the exact rule of justice. The Queen's learned Counsel do level at nothing else but that the truth may come to light how far you have offended

---

[11]An uprising in 1554 against Mary Tudor by Thomas Wyat and his followers. The plan was to replace Mary with Elizabeth.

[12]Esther, ancient queen generally known for her mildness, and famous for having thwarted a plot to kill all the Jews. Her story is told in the Old Testament book of Esther. Judith was an Old Testament heroine who saved the Jews from an Assyrian invasion by cutting off the head of the Assyrian general Holofernes.

against the Queen's person. To us full power is given to hear and examine the matter, even in your absence; yet were we desirous you should be present, lest we might seem to have derogated from your honour. We purposed not to object any thing unto you but what you were privy to, or have attempted against the Queen's person. The Letters have been read to no other purpose but to discover your offence against the Queen's person and the matters to it belonging, which are so interlaced with other matters that they cannot be severed. The whole Letters, therefore, and not parcels picked out here and there, have been openly read, for that the circumstances do give assurance what matters you dealt with Babington about.

She, interrupting him, said, The circumstances may be proved, but never the fact. Her integrity depended, not upon the credit and memory of her Secretaries, though she knew them to be honest and sincere men. Yet if they have confessed anything out of fear of torments or hope of reward and impunity, it was not to be admitted, for just causes which she would alledge elsewhere. Men's minds (said she) are diversely carried about with affections, and they would never have confessed such matters against her but for their own advantage and hope. Letters may be directed to others than those to whom they are written, and many things have been often inserted which she never dictated. If her papers had not been taken away, and she had her Secretary, she could better confute the things objected against her.

But nothing, said the Lord Treasurer, shall be objected but since the 19th day of June; neither will your Papers avail you, seeing your Secretaries and Babington himself, being never put to the rack have affirmed that you sent those Letters to Babington, which, though you deny, yet whether more credit is to be given to an affirmation than to a negation, let the Commissioners judge. But to return to the matter, this which followeth I tell you as a counsellor; Many things you have propounded time after time concerning your liberty; that they have failed of success, it is long of you, or of the Scots, and not of the Queen. For the Lords of Scotland flatly refused to deliver the King in hostage. And when the last Treaty was holden concerning your liberty, Parry was sent privily by Morgan, a dependant of yours, to murder the Queen.

Ah (said she), you are my adversary. Yea (said he) I am adversary to Queen Elizabeth's adversaries. But hereof enough; let us now proceed to Proofs. Which, when she refused to hear; Yet we (said he) will hear them; and I also (said she) will hear them in another place, and defend myself.

Now were read again her Letters to Charles Paget, . . .

As these Letters were in reading she interposed these Speeches: That Babington and her Secretaries had accused her to excuse themselves;

that she never heard of the six Executioners, and that the rest made nothing to the purpose. . . . As for her Secretaries, seeing they had done contrary to their duty and allegiance sworn unto her, they deserved no credit. They which have once foresworn themselves, though they swear again with never so great oaths and protestations, are not to be credited. Neither did these men think themselves bounden by any oath whatsoever in court of conscience, forasmuch as they had sworn their fidelity and secrecy to her before, and were no subjects of England. That Nau had many times written otherwise than she had dictated unto him, and Curle wrote whatsoever Nau bade him. But for her part she was willing to bear the burden of their fault in all things, but what might lay a blot upon her honour. And haply also they confessed these things to save themselves; supposing that they could not hurt her by confessing, who they thought should be more favourably dealt withal as being a Queen. As for Ballard, she never heard of any such, but of one Hallard [Ballard?], which had offered her his help; which notwithstanding, she had refused, for that she had heard that the same man had also vowed his service to Walsingham.

Afterwards were read certain brief Notes of her Letters to Mendoza, which Curle had confessed he had written in privy Cipher. . . .

Out of these she was pressed as if she had purposed to convey her Right in the kingdom to the Spaniard, and that Allen and Parsons lay now at Rome for that cause. She complaining that her Secretaries had broken their allegiance bound by oath, answered, When being prisoner, I languished in cares without hope of liberty, and was without all hope to effect those things which very many expected at my hands, declining now through age and sickness; it seemed good to some that the Succession of the Crown of England should be established in the Spaniard, or some English Catholic. And a Book was sent unto me to avow the Spaniard's Title; which, when it was not allowed by me, I incurred displeasure among some. But now all my hope in England being desperate, I am fully resolved not to reject foreign aid.

The Solicitor put the Commissioners in mind what would become of them, their honours, estates, and posterities if the kingdom were so conveyed. But the Lord Treasurer showed that the kingdom of England could not be conveyed, but was to descend by right of succession according to the laws; and asked her if she would any more.

She required that she might be heard in a full Parliament, or that she might in person speak with the Queen, who would (she hoped) have regard of a Queen, and with the Council. And now rising up with great confidence of countenance, she had some conference with the Lord Treasurer, Hatton, Walsingham, and the Earl of Warwick, by themselves apart.

7

ELIZABETH TUDOR

Speeches to Parliament

1586

After Mary Stuart was found guilty of conspiring to kill Elizabeth Tudor and usurp her throne, Elizabeth's Parliament began to pressure the English queen to sentence Mary to death. Elizabeth was deeply torn. Fear for her life countered fear of retaliation by the Catholic countries that supported Mary; love of her Protestant subjects vied with her blood bond with Mary, who was moreover another anointed queen, like Elizabeth herself. Parliament was adamant from the start, and after days of loud and virtually unanimous discussion among its members issued a joint supplication begging Elizabeth to defend them by sentencing Mary to "that due punishment, which by justice, and the laws of this your realm, she hath so often and so many ways for her most wicked and detestable offences deserved."

Elizabeth responded in such a way as to buy more time for herself. Her speech is thus full of paradoxes. Its language is sometimes submissive, as she expresses gratitude for her subjects' love, and sometimes imperious, as she reminds those subjects that the decision before her is "of greatest consequence" and she is not to be rushed. Similarly, Elizabeth identifies herself sometimes with Mary (a princess "of like estate") and sometimes with her people ("I see your danger in me"). Every word of Elizabeth's speech is charged with the almost unbearable tension of the moment. Nor did her speech resolve that tension. It ends only with Elizabeth promising her audience "whatever the best subjects may expect at the hands of the best princes." What that "whatever" might be, she cleverly does not say.

First Speech

So many and so great are the bottomless graces, and immeasurable benefits bestowed upon me by the Almighty, that I must not only most humbly acknowledge them as benefits, but admire them as miracles, being in no sort able to express them. And though there liveth not any that may more

---

William Cobbett, ed. *Cobbett's Parliamentary History of England* (London: R. Bagshaw, 1806–1812).

justly acknowledge himself bound to God than I, whose life He hath miraculously preserved from so many dangers, yet am I not more deeply bound to give Him thanks for any one thing, than for this which I will now tell you, and which I account as a miracle. Namely, that as I came to the crown with the most hearty good-will of all my subjects, so now after 28 years reign, I perceive in them the same, if not greater good-will towards me; which if I once lose, well might I breathe, but never think I lived. And now though my life hath been dangerously shot at, yet I protest there is nothing hath more grieved me, than that one not differing from me in sex, of like rank and degree, of the same stock, and most nearly allied unto me in blood, hath fallen into so great a crime. And so far have I been from bearing her any ill-will, that upon the discovery of certain treasonable practices against me, I wrote unto her secretly, that if she would confess them by a private letter unto myself, they should be wrapped up in silence. Neither did I write thus in mind to entrap her, for I knew then as much as she could confess. And even yet, though the matter be come thus far, if she would truly repent, and no man would undertake her cause against me, and if my life alone depended hereupon, and not the safety and welfare of my whole people, I would (I protest unfeignedly) most willingly pardon her. Nay, if England might by my death attain a more flourishing estate, and a better prince, I would most gladly lay down my life. For, for your sakes it is, and for my people's, that I desire to live. As for me, I see no such great cause why I should either be fond to live, or fear to die. I have had good experience of this world, and I know what it is to be a subject, and what to be a sovereign. Good neighbours I have had, and I have met with bad; and in trust I have found treason. I have bestowed benefits upon ill deservers; and where I have done well, have been ill requited. While I call to mind these things past, behold things present, and expect things to come, I hold them happiest that go hence soonest. Nevertheless against such mischiefs as these, I put on a better courage than is common to my sex, so as whatsoever befall me, death shall not take me unprepared.— And as touching these Treasons, I will not so prejudicate myself, or the laws of my kingdom, as not but to think that she having been the contriver of the same treasons, was bound and liable to the ancient laws, though the late act had never been made, which notwithstanding was no ways made to prejudice her. So far was it from being made to entrap her, that it was rather intended to forewarn and terrify her from attempting any thing against it. But seeing it was now in force of a law, I thought good to proceed against her according to the same. But you lawyers are so curious in scanning the nice points of the law, and following of precedents, and form, rather than expounding the laws themselves, that by exact observing of your form, she must have been indicted in Staffordshire, and have holden up her hand at the bar, and have been tried by a jury of twelve men. A proper course forsooth of trial against a Princess! To avoid therefore such absurdities, I thought it better to refer the examination of so weighty a cause to a good number of the noblest personages of the land, and the judges of the realm; and all little enough. For we princes are set as it were upon stages, in the sight and view of all the world. The least spot is soon spied in our garments, a blemish quickly noted in our doings. It behoveth us therefore to be careful that our proceedings be just and honourable. But I must tell you one thing, that by this last Act of Parliament you have brought me to a narrow streight, that I must give order for her death, which is a princess most nearly allied unto me in blood, and whose practices against me have stricken me into so great grief, that I have been glad to absent myself from this Parliament, lest I should increase my sorrow by hearing it spoken of, and not out of fear of any danger, as some think. But yet I will now tell you a secret (though it is well known that I have the property to keep counsel). It is not long since these eyes of mine saw and read an oath, wherein some bound themselves to kill me within a month: Hereby I see your danger in me, which I will be very careful to avoid. Your Association for my safety I have not forgotten, which I never so much as thought of, till a great number of hands, with many obligations, were shewed me; which as I do acknowledge as a strong argument of your true hearts, and great zeal to my safety, so shall my bond be stronger tied to a greater care for your good. But forasmuch as this matter now in hand is very rare, and of greatest consequence, I hope you do not look for any present resolution; for my manner is, in matters of less moment than this, to deliberate long upon that which is once to be resolved. In the mean time I beseech Almighty God to illuminate my mind, that I may foresee that which may serve for the good of His Church, the prosperity of the Commonwealth, and your safety. And that delay may not breed danger, we will signify our resolution with all conveniency. And whatever the best subjects may expect at the hands of the best princes, that expect from me to be performed to the full.

[*After twelve days of deliberation, Elizabeth still had not come to a decision about whether to put Mary Queen of Scots to death. Her Lord Chancellor, Bromley, and the Speaker of the House of Commons, John Puckering, approached her with an even more urgent detailed petition than the one that had been delivered before, representing Mary to Elizabeth as "greedy of your death" and reminding their queen that the Stuart queen's "friends" also "hold invasion unprofitable while you live, and therefore in their opinion your death is first and principally to be sought, as the most compendious way to ruin the realm by invasion." Mary was likened to the most "wicked queens" of the Old Testament, and Elizabeth chastised as a bad mother to the political "children" who needed her protection.*

Elizabeth's rejoinder was as equivocal as her first speech, but some of the rhetorical assurance that characterized its predecessor here seems to be missing. There is a long reverie on Elizabeth's own earlier experiences of danger, perhaps to remind her audience that she survived them, and she tries to identify herself with the ancient leaders Alcibiades and Solomon, perhaps because all imagery of queens now seemed tainted by association with Mary. She ends by confessing her speech an "answer answerless" to the hardest question of her life, and seems to have been unsatisfied with what she said, since she later polished and readjusted many of her own words before they were published.]

Second Speech

Full grievous is that way whose going on and end, yield nothing but cumber for the hire of a laborious journey. I have this day been in greater conflict with myself than ever in my life whether I should speak or hold my peace. If I speak and not complain, I shall dissemble; and if I should be silent your labour taken were all in vain. If I should complain, it might seem strange and rare; yet I confess that my most hearty desire was that some other means might have been devised to work your security and my safety, than this which is now propounded. So as I cannot but complain, though not of you, yet unto you; that I perceive by your petitions that my safety dependeth wholly upon the death of another. If there be any that think I have prolonged the time of purpose to make a counterfeit show of clemency, they do me the most undeserved wrong, as He knoweth, which is the searcher of the most secret thoughts of the heart. Or, if there be any that be persuaded that the Commissioners durst not pronounce other sentence, as fearing thereby to displease me, or to seem to fail of their care for my safety, they but heap upon me most injurious conceits. For either those, whom I have put in trust, have failed of their duties, or else they signified unto the Commissioners in my name, that my will and pleasure was that every one should deal freely according to his conscience, and what they would not openly declare that they should reveal unto me in private. It was of my most favourable mind towards her that I desired some other means might be found out to prevent this mischief. But since now it is resolved that my surety is most desperate without her death, I have a most inward feeling of sorrow, that I, which have in my time pardoned so many rebels, winked at so many treasons, or neglected them with silence, must now seem to show cruelty upon so great a princess. I have since I came to the Crown of this realm seen many defamatory Books and Pamphlets against me, accusing me to be a tyrant; well fare the writers' hearts, I believe their meaning was to tell me news; and news, indeed, it was to me to be branded with the note of tyranny; I would it were as great news to hear of their impiety. But what is it which they will not write now, when they shall hear that I have given consent, that the executioner's hands shall be imbrued in the blood of my nearest kinswoman? But so far am I from cruelty that to save mine own life I would not offer her violence; neither have I been so careful how to prolong mine own life as how to preserve both, which that it is now impossible I grieve exceedingly. I am not so void of judgment as not to see mine own perils before mine eyes, nor so mad to sharpen a sword to cut mine own throat, nor so careless as not to provide for the safety of mine own life. But this I consider with myself, that many a man would put his own life in danger to save a princess's life. I do not say so will I; yet have I many times thought upon it. But, seeing so many have both written and spoken against me, give me leave, I pray you, to say somewhat in mine own defence that ye may see what manner of woman I am, for whose safety you have passed such careful thoughts; wherein as I do with most thankful heart consider your vigilant care, so am I sure I shall never requite it had I as many lives as you all. When first I took the sceptre I was not unmindful of God the giver, and therefore began my reign with His service and the religion I had been both born in, bred in, and I trust shall die in. And though I was not ignorant how many perils I should be beset withal at home for altering religion, and how many great princes abroad, of a contrary profession, would attempt all hostility against me, yet was I no whit dismayed, knowing that God, whom only I respected, would defend both me and my cause. Hence it is that so many treacheries and conspiracies have been attempted against me that I rather marvel that I am, than muse that I should not be, were it not that God's holy hand hath protected me beyond all expectation. Then to the end I might make the better progress in the art of swaying the sceptre I entered into long and serious cogitation what things were worthy and fitting for kings to do; and I found it most necessary that they should be abundantly furnished with those special virtues, justice, temperance, prudence, and magnanimity. As for the two latter I will not boast myself; my sex doth not permit it; but for the two former I dare say (and that without ostentation) I never made a difference of persons where right was one; I never preferred for favour whom I thought not fit for worth; I never bent my ear to credit a tale that was first told, nor was so rash to corrupt my judgment with prejudice, before I heard the cause. I will not say but many reports might haply be brought me in too much favour of the one side or the other; for we princes cannot hear all ourselves; yet this I dare say boldly, my judgment went ever with the truth according to my understanding. And as full well Alcibiades[1] wished his friend not to give any answer till he had run over the letters of the alphabet; so have I not used rash and sudden resolutions in anything. And, therefore, as touching your counsels and consultations, I acknowledge them to be so careful, provident, and profitable for the preservation of my life, and to proceed from minds so sincere and to me most devoted, that I shall endeavour myself all I can, to give you cause to think your pains not ill-bestowed, and strive to make myself worthy of such subjects.

And now for your Petition, I pray you for this present to content yourselves with an Answer without Answer. Your judgment I condemn not, neither do I mistake your Reasons, but pray you to accept my thankfulness, excuse my doubtfulness, and take in good part my answer answerless. If I should say I would not do what you request I might say perhaps more than I think: And if I should say I would do it, I might plunge myself into peril, whom you labour to preserve; which in your wisdoms and discretions ye would not that I should, if ye consider the circumstances of place, time, and the manners and conditions of men.

8

ROBERT WYNGFIELD

A Circumstantial Account of the Execution of Mary Queen of Scots

1587

Many witnesses attended Mary Stuart's beheading on the morning of February 8, 1587, and several of them sent descriptions of the event back to London. Of these, the "Circumstantial Account" of the otherwise obscure Robert Wyngfield has become the most famous. It is also the most lurid—balanced

---

[1]Ancient Athenian general and statesman.

Robert Wyngfield, . . . *The Execution of Mary Queen of Scots*. From *Clarendon Historical Society Reprints* (Clarendon: Clarendon Historical Society, 1886), vol. VIII. First published London, 1752.

in some ways, but in others an excellent example of how easily Mary Stu-
art's story was absorbed into propaganda. Many of its details have become
legendary, particularly that of the headpiece that allegedly slipped off when
the queen's severed head was held aloft and the "little dog, which was crept
under her clothes" as she knelt and "would not be gotten forth but with force;
and afterwards would not depart from the dead corpse."

Wyngfield apparently produced his "Circumstantial Account" for his dis-
tant relation, Elizabeth's treasurer, Lord Burghley, and though the account
was initially intended for Burghley's eyes only, its fine attention to detail
eventually made it the official report of the execution. It was often reprinted
as such.

It may please your good Lordship to be advertised that, according as your Honour gave me in command, I have here set down in writing the true order and manner of the execution of the Lady Mary, last Queen of Scots, the 8th of February last, in the great hall within the castle of Fotheringay, together with relation of all such speeches and actions spoken and done by the said Queen, or any other, and all other circumstances and proceedings concerning the same and after the delivery of the said Scottish Queen . . . unto the end of the said execution, as followeth:

It being certified the 6th of February last, to the said Queen, . . . that she was to prepare herself to die the 8th of February next, she seemed not to be in any terror, for ought that appeared by any of her outward gesture or behavior (other than marvelling she should die), but rather with smiling cheer and pleasing countenance she accepted the said admonition of preparation to her (as she said) unexpected execution, saying that her death should be welcome unto her, seeing her Majesty was so resolved, and that her soul were too far unworthy the fruition of the joys of Heaven forever, whose body would not in this world be content to endure the stroke of the executioner for a moment. And that spoken, she wept bitterly and became silent.

The said 8th day of February being come, and time and place appointed for the execution, the Queen—being of stature tall, of body corpulent, round-shouldered, her face fat and broad, double-chinned, and hazel-eyed, her borrowed hair aborne—her attire was this: On her head she had a dressing of lawn,[1] edged with bone lace, a pomander chain and an *Agnus Dei*[2] about her neck, a crucifix in her hand, a pair

---

[1]A sheer, fine linen or cotton fabric.
[2]Small carved lamb meant to recall Christ (the Lamb of God).

of beads at her girdle, with a golden cross at the end of them, a veil of lawn fastened to her caul,[3] bowed out with wire, and edged round about with bone-lace, her gown was of black satin printed, with a train and her sleeves to the ground, with acorn buttons of jet, trimmed with pearl, and short sleeves of satin, black cut, with a pair of sleeves of purple velvet whole under them, her girdle whole, of figured black satin, and her petticoat skirts of crimson velvet, her shoes of Spanish leather with the rough side outward, a pair of green silk garters, her nether stockings worsted color watch-clocked with silver, and edged on the top with silver, and next her leg a pair of Jersey hose, white, &c. Thus appareled, she departed her chamber, and willingly bended her steps toward the place of execution.

As the Commissioners, and divers other Knights, were meeting the Queen coming forth, one of her servants, called Melvin, kneeling on his knees to his Queen and Mistress, wringing hands and shedding tears, used these words unto her: "Ah! Madam, unhappy me, what man on Earth was ever before the messenger of so important sorrow and heaviness as I shall be, when I shall report that my good and gracious Queen and Mistress is beheaded in England?" This said, his tears prevented him any further speaking; whereupon the said Queen, pouring forth her dying tears, thus answered him:

"My good Servant, cease to lament, for thou hast cause rather to joy than to mourn, for now shall thou see Mary Stuart's troubles receive their long expected end, and determination, for know," said she, "good servant, all the world is but vanity, and subject still to more sorrow, than a whole ocean of tears can bewail. But I pray thee," said she, "carry this message from me, that I die a true woman to my religion, and like a true Queen of Scotland and France, but God forgive them," said she, "that have long desired my end, and thirsted for my blood, as the hart doth for the water brooks. Oh God," said she, "to show thou art the anchor of truth, and truth itself, knowest the inward chamber of my thought, how that I was ever willing that England and Scotland should be united together. Well," said she, "commend me to my son, and tell him, that I have not done any thing prejudicial to the State and Kingdom of Scotland." And so resolving herself again into tears, [she] said, "Good Melvin, farewell," and with weeping eyes, and her cheeks all besprinkled with tears, as they were, kissed him, saying once again, "Farewell good Melvin, and pray for thy Mistress and Queen."

And then she turned herself unto the Lords, and told them she had

---

[3]A head covering of net.

certain requests to make unto them. One was for certain money to be paid to Curle, her servant. Sir Amias Paulet, knowing of that money, answered to this effect, it should. "Next, that her poor servants might have that with quietness which she had given them by her will, and that they might be favourably intreated,[4] and to send them safely into their countries." To this (said she), "I conjure you as that it would please the Lords, to permit her poor distressed servants to be present about her at her death, that their eyes and hearts may see and witness how patiently their Queen and Mistress would endure her execution, and so make relation when they came into their country, that she died a true constant Catholic to her religion."

Then the Earl of Kent did answer thus: "Madam, that which you have desired, cannot conveniently be granted, for if it should, it were to be feared that some of them, with speeches or other behaviour, would both be grievous to your Grace, and troublesome and unpleasing to us and our company, whereof we have had some experience, they would not stick to put some superstitious trumpery in practice, and if it were but in dipping their handkerchiefs in your Grace's blood, whereof it were very unmeets[5] for us to give allowance."

"My Lords," said the Queen of Scots, "I will give my word although it be but dead, that they shall not deserve any blame in the actions you have named, but alas (poor souls) it would do them good to bid their mistress farewell; and I hope your mistress (meaning the Queen), being a maiden queen, will vouch for my regard of womanhood, that I shall have some of my own people about me at my death, and I know her Majesty hath not given you any such straight charge or commission, but that you might grant me a request of far greater courtesy than this is, if I were a woman of far meaner calling than the Queen of Scots." And then perceiving that she could not obtain her request without some difficulty, burst out into tears, saying:

"I am cousin to your Queen, and descended from the blood royal of Henry VII, and a married queen of France, and an anointed queen of Scotland." Then upon great consultation had betwixt the two Earls, and others in commission, it was granted to her, what she instantly before earnestly intreated; and desired her to make choice of six of her best beloved men and women. . . . Then with an unappalled countenance, without any terror of the place, the persons, or the preparations, she came out of the entry into the hall, stepped up to the scaffold, being two foot

[4]Treated.
[5]Inappropriate.

high, and twelve foot broad, with rails round about, hanged and covered with black, with a low stool, long fair cushion . . . covered also with black. The stool brought her, she sat down. The Earl of Kent stood on the right hand, and the Earl of Shrewsbury on the other; other knights and gentlemen stood about the rails.

The commission for her execution was read, . . . which done, the people with a loud voice said, God save the Queen. During the reading of this commission, the said Queen was very silent, listening unto it with so careless a regard, as if it had not concerned her at all; nay, rather with so merry and cheerful a countenance, as if it had been a pardon from her Majesty for her life, and withal used such a strangeness in her words, as if she had not known any of the assembly, nor had been anything seen in the English tongue.

Then Mr. Doctor Fletcher, Dean of Peterborough, standing directly before her without the rails, bending his body with great reverence, uttered this exhortation following:

"Madame, the Queen's most excellent Majesty (whom God preserve long to reign over us), having (notwithstanding this preparation for the execution of justice justly to be done unto you, for your many trespasses against her sacred person, state, and government) a tender care over your soul, which presently departing out of your body, must either be separated in the true faith in Christ or perish forever, doth for Jesus Christ offer unto you the comfortable promises of God, wherein I beseech your Grace, even in the bowels of Jesus Christ, to consider these three Things: First, your State past, and transitory glory; secondly, your condition present of death; thirdly, your Estate to come, either in everlasting happiness or perpetual infelicity. For the first, let me speak to your Grace, with David the King, forget (Madam) yourself, and your own people, and your father's house; forget your natural birth, your royal and princely dignity, so shall the King of Kings have pleasure in your spiritual beauty, &c. Madam, even now, Madam, doth God Almighty open you a door into a heavenly Kingdom; shut not therefore this passage by the hardening of your heart, and grieve not the spirit of God, which may seal your Hope to a day of redemption."

The Queen three or four times said unto him, "Mr. Dean, trouble not yourself nor me, for know that I am settled in the ancient Catholic and Roman religion, and in defence thereof, by God's Grace I mind to spend my blood."

"Then," said Mr. Dean, "Madam, change your opinion and repent you of your former wickedness; settle your faith only upon this ground, that in Christ Jesus you hope to be saved." She answered again and again, with great earnestness, "Good Mr. Dean, trouble not yourself any more about this matter, for I was born into this religion, have lived in this religion, and resolve to die in this religion."

Then the Earls, when they saw how far unconformable she was under Mr. Dean's good exhortations, said, "Madam, we will pray for your Grace with Mr. Dean, that you may have your mind lightened with the true knowledge of God and his word."

"My Lords," answered the Queen, "if you will pray with me, I will even from my heart thank you, and think myself greatly favoured by you; but to join in prayer with you in your manner, who are not of one religion with me, it were a sin, and I will not."

Then the Lords called Mr. Dean again, and bade him say on, or what he thought good else: The Dean kneeled and prayed . . .

All the assembly, save the Queen and her servants, said the prayer after Mr. Dean as he spake it, during which prayer the Queen sat upon her stool, having her *Agnus Dei*, crucifix, beads,[6] and an office in Latin. Thus furnished with superstitious trumpery, not regarding what Mr. Dean said, she began very fastly with tears and a loud voice to pray in Latin, and in the midst of her prayers, with overmuch weeping and mourning slipped off her stool, and kneeling presently said divers other Latin prayers.

Then she rose and kneeled down again, praying in English for Christ's afflicted church, an end of her troubles, for her son, and for the Queen's majesty, to God for forgiveness of the sins of them in this island. She forgave her enemies with all her heart, that had long sought her blood. This done, she desired all saints to make intercession for her to the saviour of the world, Jesus Christ. Then she began to kiss her crucifix, and to cross herself, saying these words: "Even as thy arms, oh Jesu Christ, were spread here upon the cross, so receive me, so receive me into the arms of mercy."

Then the two executioners kneeled down unto her, desiring her to forgive them her death. She answered, "I forgive you with all my heart; for I hope this death shall give an end to all my troubles."

They, with her two women helping, began to disrobe her, and then she laid the crucifix upon the stool. One of the executioners took from her neck the *Agnus Dei*, and she laid hold of it, saying she would give it to one of her women, and withal told the executioner that he should have money for it. Then they took off her chain, [and] she made herself

[6]Rosary.

unready[7] with a kind of gladness, and, smiling, putting on a pair of sleeves with her own hands, which the two executioners before had rudely put off, and with such speed, as if she had longed to be gone out of the world.

During the disrobing of this Queen she never altered her countenance; but, smiling, said she never had such grooms before to make her unready, nor ever did put off her clothes before such company. At length, unattired and unapparelled to her petticoat and girdle, the two women burst out into a great and pitiful shrieking, crying, and lamentation, crossed themselves, and prayed in Latin. The Queen turned towards them, embraced them, and said these words in French, "Ne criez vous, j'ai prier pour vous,"[8] and so crossed, and kissed them, and bade them pray for her. Then with a smiling countenance she turned to her men servants, Melvin and the rest, crossed them, bade them farewell, and pray for her to the last.

One of the women having a Corpus Christi cloth,[9] lapped it up three cornerwise, kissed it, and put it over the face of the Queen, and pinned it fast upon the caul of her head. Then the two women departed. The Queen kneeled down on the cushion resolutely, and without any token of fear of death, said aloud in Latin the Psalm, *In te domine confido.*[10] Then, groping for the block, she laid down her head, putting her chain over her back with both her hands, which holding there still had been cut off, had they not been espied. Then she laid herself upon the block most quietly, and stretching out her arms and legs cried out, *In manus tuus, Domine, commendo spiritum meum,* three or four times.[11]

At last while one of the executioners held her straightly with one of his hands, the other gave two strokes with an axe before he did cut off her head, and yet left a little gristle behind.

She made very small noise; no part stirred form the place where she lay. The executioners lifted up the head, and bade "God save the Queen." Then her dressing of lawn fell from her head, which appeared as gray as if she had been threescore and ten years old, polled very short, her face much altered. Her lips stirred up and down almost a quarter of an hour after her head was cut off. Then said Mr. Dean, "So perish all the Queen's enemies." The Earl of Kent came to the dead body, and with a lower voice said, "Such end happen to all the Queen's and gospel's enemies."

One of the executioners plucking off her garters espied her little dog,

---

[7]Undressed.
[8]"Do not cry; I have prayed for you."
[9]Cloth reputedly from the shroud of Christ.
[10]I trust in you, oh God.
[11]Into your hands, oh God, I commend my spirit.

which was crept under her clothes, which would not be gotten forth but with force; and afterwards would not depart from the dead corpse, but came and lay between her head and shoulders, a thing much noted. The dog, imbrued in her blood, was carried away and washed, as all things else were that had any blood, save those things which were burned. The executioners were sent away with money for their fees, not having any one thing that belonged unto her.

Afterwards, everyone was commanded forth of the hall, saving the sheriff and his men, who carried her up into a great chamber, made ready for the surgeons to embalm her, and there she was embalmed.

And thus, I hope, my very good Lord, I have certified your Honour of all actions, matters, and circumstances as did pass from her, or any other at her death. Wherein I dare promise your good Lordship (if not in some better or worse words thereof spoken I am somewhat mistaken) in matter I have not in any wise offended. Howbeit, I will not so justify my duties herein, but that many things might well have been omitted as not worthy mention. Yet, because it is your Lordship's fault to desire to know all, and I have certified all, it is an offence pardonable. So resting at your Honour's further commandment, I take my leave this 11th of February. . . .

9

ADAM BLACKWOOD

The History of Mary Queen of Scots

1587

Adam Blackwood was a Scot, a Catholic, a lawyer, and a poet. He also ranks with John Leslie, Bishop of Ross, among Mary Stuart's staunchest advocates. Blackwood spent almost all of his adult life in France, where he wrote numerous diatribes against Elizabeth and defenses of Mary's virtue that far surpass Leslie's in their combative tone. Blackwood's monumental history of Mary's life and death, Martyre de la royne d'Escosse, *was originally published in Paris, then translated from French into English as* The History

Adam Blackwood, *The History of Mary Queen of Scots, a Fragment.* Ed. and trans. Alexander Macdonald (Edinburgh: Maitland Club 31, 1834). First published as *Martyre de la royne d'Escosse* (Paris, 1587).

of Mary Queen of Scots. *Especially on the European continent, the work was destined to shape Mary's saintly image.*

As his original title promises, Blackwood casts Mary as a Catholic martyr, and his engorged, graphic prose leaves his reader with little choice but to abhor the butchery at Fotheringay. Although not present at the execution, he claimed as sources English and French reports of that event, bolstered with the testimonies of Mary's own servants. Blackwood's Martyre *was first published anonymously and went into at least five editions in only two years. Part of its aim was to inspire James VI of Scotland to avenge his mother's death, and while obviously it fell short of that end, the work remains an important record of Mary Stuart's life . . . and a testament to the depth of devotion she could inspire.*

. . . The place of execution was in a great parlour, in the midst whereof a scaffold was set up, twelve foot square and two foot high, spread over with black cotton, towards the which her Majesty mounted so nimbly that she seemed to have no fear of death, neither ever changed her countenance. And now being come up, she rested herself a little, and presently beginneth to speak to the officers of her cruel cousin Elizabeth, entreating them to permit her to have her almoner[1] to come to her, to comfort her in her God, and to receive of him some comfortable instruction, together with the holy sacrament, before her departure out of this vale of misery.

The Earl of Kent answered, that he was sorry for her to see her so much given to the superstitions of the times past, and that it were better for her to carry the cross of Christ in heart, not in her hand.

To whom she replied, that it was to little purpose to carry such an object in her hand, if the heart were not touched inwardly with earnest motion and remembrance of his bitter death and passion which he suffered upon the cross for miserable man's sin, that died upon the cross. I think it (saith she) a thing most fit for every true Christian, to have it to put them in remembrance of their redemption purchased by Christ, but especially they at that time, when death threatneth.

But seeing by no means she could have her almoner, as she was promised, she made another motion to them, that all her servants might be present to be eyewitness of her constancy in true piety; which, after she had instantly desired and promised that she would command and enjoin them silence, so that their crying, weeping and lamentations should be no hindrance or trouble to her in her death, they granted her

[1]A person, usually clerical, who distributes alms for another.

that two of her maids of honor should come. But one of them at her entry in the place of execution, seeing her dear mistress so forwardly in preparation for the butcher's hands, could not contain herself from weeping and from pitiful moan, and fell down as dead for a time, whom, when her mistress perceived to have recovered her senses, . . . by a sign made to her by her finger upon the mouth, enjoined her silence; at the sign of which she forced herself to contain her lament.

This done, the two maids together mount up upon the scaffold to do their mistress the last charitable service, and that with watery eyes and sorrowful hearts. They began to help her to take away her mask, her coif, and other ornaments. But the shameless executioner could, by no entreaty her Majesty could make, nor yet reward, be moved to withhold his helping hands. Neither did any of Elizabeth's officers forbid him: For after her Majesty's gown was stripped down to the middle, he snatched her rudely by the arms and pulled off her doublet, her straight bodice, which [was] low in the collar, so that her neck, being all naked, appeared to the spectators more white than snow or alabaster.

This done, the cruel butcher kneeleth down, asking her forgiveness. "Do thy office in the name of God; thou art but an instrument. I forgive thee with all my heart, and all others that be the authors of my death, even with as good will as I desire my own sins to be forgiven me at God's hands."

She protested likewise, in all the beholders' presence, that she never had attempted anything against the life or state of her cousin, nor committed anything worthy of blame, either for the overthrow of religion or the commonwealth. If they did impute her constancy in her religion as a fault worthy of death, let them look to it, who never had any care to instruct and inform her otherwise, all the long time of my twenty years' captivity. I hope shortly to be in Paradise with my dear saviour, Jesus Christ, for whose obedience made for me I doubt not to shed my blood, even to the last drop. I count myself more happy now to die in a right mind to end my misery, than to live longer, enduring the daily reproaches of my enemies, worse than a bitter death, than to attend any longer till nature, thus fainting, did finish the course of her life, when she should not be right in her senses, and perfect remembrance of her duty towards God and her neighbour. She said, she hoped in him, of whom that cross she carried in her hand put her in remembrance, and before whose feet she prostrated herself in soul and body, that he would receive her into eternal glory. . . . She protested, as before, in all the auditories' hearing, that she was innocently accused, charged and condemned of such things she never thought on, and hoped the loss of this temporal life should be the passage, beginning and entrance to life eternal, with the holy angels and the souls of [the] blessed, that should receive her soul and innocent blood, and represent it before God, for a deduction of all her sins and offences. She besought them all to pray for her, that God would hear her, and that she might obtain grace and pardon.

These were her prayers, being upon her knees upon the scaffold, praying also for the Pope, the kings of France, Spain, the Queen of England, and the King of Scotland, her dear son, that God would enlighten them all with his spirit, and direct them in the truth, and that he would take pity upon his church militant, and turn away his anger from the isle of Great Britain, which she did perceive he threatened with scourges for the abominable, willful impiety committed by the inhabitants.

She thus likewise prayed at her first entry upon the scaffold, and after reiterated the same three several times. But the Dean of Peterborough, Dr. Fletcher, did what he could to interrupt her, whom she entreated not to trouble her, for she was fully resolved how to die, without any counsel from him or any of his sort. He could give her no further contentment for her soul than she had already, for she did anchor her on Christ; and for the people, they could give her no further comfort.

This notwithstanding, the Dean continued in his prayers, and she proceeded likewise forward, praying in Latin, lifting up her voice above his so loud that all being present did clearly hear her. She had a golden cross about her neck having the image of our Saviour, which, prayer being ended, she would have given to one of her maids. But the butcher snatched at it, and would not suffer her, albeit her Majesty did earnestly intreat, offering him that her maid should give him thrice the value of it, but no remedy. He would not let her have it.

All being ready, she taketh her last farewell of her maids, and kissed them courteously, thanking them for their faithful services, bidding them adieu, and bade them retire themselves quietly, giving them her last blessing, and making the sign of the cross over them; but perceiving one of them could not hold, but burst forth into tears, she commanded [her] to hold her peace, and to keep silence, telling her that she had passed her promise that she and the other maid should not be troublesome to her in her death. She bade them both retire themselves soberly, and to pray to God for her, now they could do her no more good. This done, she fell down upon her knees, without giving the least sign or demonstration of discontent or fear of death. Her constancy and boldness of spiritual courage, her confidence and assurance of hope of recompense of eternal life, of God, in lieu and place of her momentary afflictions, now to be enjoyed of her, was such that all the assistants—yea, her hardest-hearted enemies—were greatly moved; and it was credibly reported of many that were present, that amongst all the whole company there was only two or three persons that could withhold weeping, they esteemed the spectacle so strange, condemning these in their conscience who were the authors of such a cruelty which, in former times, they never heard nor read of the like. She commends finally her soul to the tuition of the Almighty, in these words of the psalm, saying often and reiterating the words, *"In manus tuus, Domine, commendo spiritum meum,"*[2] and that with a loud voice, far surmounting the Dean in the ears of the assistants.

In the meanwhile, the butcher gave her a great blow with the axe, whereby he pierced the strings within her head, which he struck not of but at the third blow, to make her martyrdom the more noble, albeit it well is known that not the pain, or the punishment, but the cause maketh the martyr. After he had done, he hastily snatcheth up the head in his hand, and showing it to the assistants, said, "God save Queen Elizabeth, and so befall all the enemies of the gospel," although there were no other that favoured the gospel, and that lived as the gospel directed but Elizabeth. But howsoever in outward show, she made a cloak for her wicked life of the sacred gospel, which thereby she profaned. Yet if her life were weighed in just and even balance, it should be found (if all things were clearly known and censured accordingly) she should become behind and be postponed this holy martyr by many degrees.

After, in derision and contempt, he pulled off her coif and shewed her white hairs, with contemptuous words unworthy to be spoken or heard by the mouth or ears of any Christian. He pointed also to the crown of her head, to shew it to the people, because it was newly shaven, which she was constrained to do by reason of a grievous rheum[3] which troubled her often.

The tragedy ended, the poor maids, careful of the honour of their mistress, humbly besought and prayed Paulet the cruel jailor, that the butcher might have no more ado with their sovereign lady's body, and that it might be permitted them to disattire her body when all the people were departed the place, that no further indignity might be offered her sacred Majesty's corpse, seeing all malice, hatred, envy, and contempt of the dead ought to end after their decease. They promised him her apparel, and all that was about her, and whatsoever besides he would demand in reason, so that he would not anymore come near or handle her sacred body.

But cursed Cerberus,[4] Paulet I mean, commandeth them very rudely to depart the chamber, leaving his hellhound with the corpse to do with

---

[2]Into your hands, oh God, I commend my spirit."
[3]Rheumatism.
[4]Fierce and vicious three-headed dog who guarded the entrance to Hades in Greek myth.

what he would. He presently pulleth off her shoes and all the rest of her apparel, which as yet was left about her body, and after, when he had done what he would, the corpse was carried into a chamber next adjoining, fearing the said maids should come to do any charitable good office.

It did increase greatly their desire so to do after they did see their mistress's corpse through a little hole of the chamber wall, which was covered with cloth. But the woeful corpse was kept a long time in this chamber till it began to corrupt and smell strongly, so that in the end they were constrained to salt it, and to embalm lightly to save charges, and after to wrap it up in a cask of lead, keeping it seven months there before it was interred at Peterborough, where also Catherine of Spain[5] lay buried before.

[5]Catherine of Aragon, Henry VIII's first wife.

A Mary Queen of Scots Chronology (1542-1587)

1509 Death of Henry VII; accession of Henry VIII

1516 Birth of Mary Tudor, to Henry VIII and Catherine of Aragon

1517 Traditional beginning of Protestant Reformation

1532 Excommunication of Henry VIII and founding of Church of England

1533 Marriage of Henry VIII and Anne Boleyn; birth of Elizabeth Tudor

1536 Beheading of Anne Boleyn

1537 Birth of Edward VI

1542 Birth of Mary Stuart to James V of Scotland and Marie de Guise

Death of James V and accession of Mary Stuart to throne of Scotland

1547 Death of Henry VIII; accession of Edward VI in England (House of Tudor)

Death of Francois I; accession of Henri II in France (House of Valois)

1548 Mary Stuart sent to France

1553 Death of Edward VI; accession of Mary Tudor

Return of English church to Roman Catholicism

1554 Elizabeth Tudor imprisoned in Tower of London for suspected involvement in Protestant rebellion against Mary Tudor

1558 Death of Mary Tudor; accession of Elizabeth I in England

Marriage of Mary Stuart and François II, crown prince of France

John Knox's *First Blast of the Trumpet against the Monstrous Regiment of Women*

1559 Death of Henri II of France; accession of François II with Mary Stuart as consort

Religious settlement in England enforcing Protestant religion by law

1560 Death of François II

1561 Return of Mary Stuart to Scotland

1562 Wars of Religion begin in France

1565 Marriage of Mary Stuart and Henry, Lord Darnley

1566 Birth of Mary Stuart's son, the future James VI of Scotland

1567 Murder of Darnley; Mary Stuart elopes with James Hepburn, Lord Bothwell

Mary taken captive and forced to abdicate Scottish throne

James VI declared king of Scotland

1568 Mary Stuart flees to England

Hearing at York leads to Mary's captivity at Tutbury Castle

1569 Northern Rebellion against Elizabeth Tudor

John Leslie's *Defence of the Honour of. . . Marie*

1571 Ridolfi plot against Elizabeth Tudor detected

St. Bartholomew's Day Massacre in France

George Buchanan's *Detection of the Doings of Mary Queen of Scots*

1577 Francis Drake sails world; English colonial expansion underway

1581 English Act of Persuasions makes reconciliation to Catholic faith treason

1584 Bond of Association

1585 Act of Association

English conflict with Spain

1586 Babington Plot detected

Mary Stuart tried for treason because of alleged involvement with Babington Plot

1587 Execution of Mary Stuart

Robert Wyngfield writes *A Circumstantial Account of the Execution of Mary, Queen of Scots*

Adam Blackwood's *Martyre de la royne d'Escosse* published in France

1588 English defeat of Spanish Armada

1595 Irish insurrection against English colonial rule

1603 Death of Elizabeth Tudor; accession of James VI of Scotland as James I of England

Questions for Consideration

1. What authorities does John Knox cite in his argument against "the monstrous regiment of women"? How might these authorities be seen to contradict one another, and what does Knox's reliance on them tell us about his reading audience?

2. Compare Leslie's embrace of the possibility of female rule with Knox's diatribe against it. What are Leslie's other concerns in his *Defence of the Honour of . . . Marie* besides refuting Knox and those who shared Knox's opinion? How is Leslie's argument similar to Knox's?

3. What is Buchanan's greatest grievance against Mary Queen of Scots? What was the context of his *Detection* and how did Buchanan, via the *Detection,* seek to influence historical events?

4. The question of the succession of the English crown was one of the most difficult and vexed of the sixteenth century. Why was this question so important in Tudor England? How did it influence the actions and opinions of Elizabeth and her subjects?

5. Imagine what England might have been like if Mary Queen of Scots had indeed usurped Elizabeth's throne or merely inherited it from her. How might the country have been different, in terms of religion and foreign relations, from what it was under the Elizabethan regime? Do you think Mary's accession would necessarily have made a difference since the crown eventually passed to her son, James VI/I, anyway?

6. What was England's relationship to the rest of Europe in the second half of the sixteenth century? How was that relationship complicated by the "problem" of Mary Queen of Scots? How were England's problems in this period similar to those of other European countries, such as France and Spain? How were they distinctively different?

7. The Protestant Reformation was one of the sixteenth century's most colossally important legacies. In what ways did the resulting conflict between the Catholic and Protestant faiths manifest itself? How did that conflict affect the fortunes of kings and queens of the day, particularly Elizabeth Tudor and Mary Stuart?

8. Consider the influence of Mary's, and Elizabeth's, male subjects upon each of these queens, and upon their relationship to one another. What were the differences in the ways that Mary and Elizabeth used their womanhood? How were their concerns and strategies of gendered self-representation different? How were they similar? What political problems might have been avoided or resolved if, as Cecil and Throckmorton imagined, either Mary or Elizabeth had been a king? How might that have made matters worse?

9. The letters that passed between Mary and Elizabeth demonstrate several different ways of interpreting Mary's captivity. What were some of those ways, and do they seem to have changed over time?

10. What were Elizabeth's reasons for keeping Mary Stuart under lock and key? Why might she have avoided personal contact with her? For dramatic purposes, several plays, operas, and films have included an imaginary meeting between the two queens. What do you suppose such a meeting might have been like?

11. A common sixteenth-century assumption about women was that they were inherently disorderly, a walking challenge to divine, human, and natural law. How does this assumption shape Buchanan's *Detection* and help to give his accusations against Mary Stuart rhetorical force and authority?

12. Why did so many English Protestants hate and fear Mary Queen of Scots? Why were they so much more willing to accept—and even love—Elizabeth Tudor?

13. How did the Bond of Association directly influence Mary Stuart's fate? How did it define the relationship between Elizabeth's subjects and Elizabeth?

14. In what sense were the legal proceedings at Fotheringay Castle fair to Mary Queen of Scots and appropriate to her situation? To what extent can they be seen as unfair and inappropriate?

15. What were the most effective features of Mary Queen of Scots's defense at her treason trial? What were the least effective? Are there contradictory elements of that defense? Did Mary have a chance, given the amount and nature of the evidence against her? What was that evidence and how reliable was it?

16. Read Elizabeth's speeches closely and, on the basis of their language and what you know of their audience (Parliament), determine what Elizabeth meant and intended by them. How do the speeches bolster her authority? How do they undercut it?

17. Was Elizabeth right to sentence Mary Queen of Scots to death? If Elizabeth had kept a diary recording her dilemma over whether to sign Mary's death warrant, what might it have said?

18. In what ways was Mary Stuart's death a blow to the Catholic cause in Europe? How might it actually have helped that cause?

19. What individuals shaped Mary's ultimate fate? Could Mary herself be considered one of them? How or how not?

Selected Bibliography

SIXTEENTH-CENTURY SCOTLAND

Bain, J. et al., eds. *Calendar of State Papers Relating to Scotland and Mary Queen of Scots, 1547–1603.* 9 vols. Edinburgh, 1890–1969.

Donaldson, Gordon. *All the Queen's Men. Power and Politics in Mary Stewart's Scotland.* London: Batsford, 1983.

Ferguson, William. *Scotland's Relations with England: A Survey to 1707.* Edinburgh: John Donald Publishers, 1977.

Lynch, Michael. *Scotland: A New History.* London: Pimlico, 1991.

TUDOR ENGLAND

Dawson, Jane E. A. "William Cecil and the British Dimension of Early Elizabethan Foreign Policy." *History* 74 (1989): 196–216.

Guy, John. *Tudor England.* Oxford: Oxford University Press, 1988.

McGrath, Patrick. *Papists and Puritans under Elizabeth I.* New York: Walker and Company, 1967.

Palliser, D. M. *The Age of Elizabeth.* London: Longman, 1983.

SIXTEENTH-CENTURY EUROPE

Elton, G. R. *The New Cambridge Modern History,* vol. ii. Cambridge: Cambridge University Press, 1958.

———. *Reformation Europe, 1517–59.* London: Collins, 1963.

Mattingly, G. *Renaissance Diplomacy.* London: Jonathan Cape, 1955.

POLITICS AND PARLIAMENT IN THE REIGN OF ELIZABETH I

Dean, David. *Law-making and Society in Late Elizabethan England: The Parliament of Elizabeth, 1584–1601.* Cambridge: Cambridge University Press, 1996.

Fletcher, Anthony. *Tudor Rebellions.* London: Longman, 1983.

Haigh, Christopher, ed. *The Reign of Elizabeth I.* London: Macmillan, 1984.

Heisch, Allison. "Queen Elizabeth I: Parliamentary Rhetoric and the Exercise of Power." *Signs* 1 (1975): 31–55.

———. *Queen Elizabeth I: Political Speeches and Parliamentary Addresses, 1558–1601.* Madison: University of Wisconsin Press, 1994.

Loades, David. *Power in Tudor England.* New York: St. Martin's Press, 1997.
MacCaffrey, Wallace. *The Shaping of the Elizabethan Regime.* Princeton: Princeton University Press, 1968.
Neale, J. E. *Elizabeth and Her Parliaments.* 2 vols. London: Jonathan Cape, 1957.
Smith, Lacey Baldwin. *Treason in Tudor England: Politics and Paranoia.* Princeton: Princeton University Press, 1986.

SUCCESSION CONTROVERSY

Axton, Marie. "The Influence of Edmund Plowden's Succession Treatise." *Huntington Library Quarterly* 37 (1974): 209–26.
Levine, Mortimer. *The Early Elizabethan Succession Question, 1558–68.* Stanford: Stanford University Press, 1966.

FEMALE SOVEREIGNTY AND SIXTEENTH-CENTURY REPRESENTATIONS OF WOMEN

Axton, Marie. *The Queen's Two Bodies: Drama and the Elizabethan Succession.* London: Royal Historical Society, 1977.
Davis, Natalie Zemon. "Women on Top." In Davis, ed., *Society and Culture in Early Modern France.* Stanford: Stanford University Press, 1975.
Ferguson, Margaret, Maureen Quilligan, and Nancy J. Vickers, eds., *Rewriting the Renaissance: The Discourses of Sexual Difference in Early Modern England.* Chicago: University of Chicago Press, 1986.
Henderson, Katherine Usher and Barbara F. McManus, eds. *Half Humankind: Contexts and Texts of the Controversy about Women in England, 1540–1640.* Urbana: University of Illinois Press, 1985.
Jordan, Constance. "Women's Rule in Sixteenth-Century British Thought." *Renaissance Quarterly* 40 (Autumn 1991): 421–52.
Maclean, Ian. *The Renaissance Notion of Woman.* Cambridge: Cambridge University Press, 1980.
Prior, Mary, ed. *Women in English Society, 1500–1800.* New York: Methuen, 1985.
Woodbridge, Linda. *Woman and the English Renaissance: Literature and the Nature of Womankind, 1540–1620.* Urbana: University of Illinois Press, 1986.

LIFE AND IMAGE OF ELIZABETH I

Bassnett, Susan. *Elizabeth I: A Feminist Perspective.* Oxford: Berg, 1988.
Berry, Philippa. *Of Chastity and Power: Elizabethan Literature and the Unmarried Queen.* London: Routledge, 1989.
Frye, Susan. *Elizabeth I: The Competition for Representation.* Oxford: Oxford University Press, 1993.
Hackett, Helen. *Virgin Mother, Maiden Queen: Elizabeth I and the Cult of the Virgin Mary.* London: Macmillan, 1995.
MacCaffrey, Wallace. *Elizabeth I.* London: Edward Arnold, 1993.

Mumby, Frank. *Elizabeth and Mary Stuart.* London: Constable and Co., 1914.

Yates, Frances. *Astraea: The Imperial Theme in the Sixteenth Century.* London: Routledge, 1975.

LIFE AND IMAGE OF MARY QUEEN OF SCOTS

Collinson, Patrick. *The English Captivity of Mary Queen of Scots.* Sheffield: University of Sheffield Press, 1969.

Donaldson, Gordon. *The First Trial of Mary Queen of Scots.* New York: Stein and Day, 1969.

Fraser, Antonia. *Mary Queen of Scots.* New York: Greenwich House, 1969.

Hosack, John. *Mary Queen of Scots and Her Accusers.* Edinburgh and London: Blackwood and Sons, 1870–84.

Lynch, Michael, ed. *Mary Stewart.* London: Basil Blackwell, 1988.

Phillips, James Emerson. *Images of a Queen: Mary Stuart in Sixteenth-Century Literature.* Berkeley: University of California Press, 1964.

Plowden, Alison. *Two Queens in One Isle: The Deadly Relationship of Elizabeth I and Mary Queen of Scots.* Sussex: Harvester Press, 1984.

Smailes, Helen and Duncan Thomson. *The Queen's Image: A Celebration of Mary Queen of Scots.* Edinburgh: National Gallery of Scotland, 1987.

Wormald, Jenny. *Mary Queen of Scots: A Study in Failure.* London: George Philip, 1988.

THE TRIAL OF MARY QUEEN OF SCOTS: HISTORY AND INTERPRETATION

Gallagher, Lowell. *Medusa's Gaze; Conscience and Casuistry in the Renaissance.* Stanford: Stanford University Press, 1991.

Steuart, A. Francis. *The Trial of Mary Queen of Scots.* Edinburgh and London: William Hodge and Co., 1923.

Index